BELFAST
A CENTURY

BOVRIL

Belfast City Hall, Donegall Place, *c*. 1908

BELFAST
A CENTURY

JONATHAN BARDON

PICTURE RESEARCH

WENDY DUNBAR
HILARY BELL

THE
BLACKSTAFF
PRESS
BELFAST

For Annie Johnston
a proud citizen of Belfast
for most of the twentieth century

JB

For Dermott
Tyrone and Jordan

WD

In memory of
my mother and my father

HB

First published in 1999 by
The Blackstaff Press Limited
Blackstaff House, Wildflower Way, Apollo Road
Belfast BT12 6TA, Northern Ireland

Printed in Northern Ireland by W. & G. Baird Limited

A CIP catalogue record for this book
is available from the British Library

ISBN 0-85640-659-7

Mickey Marley's roundabout, Pound Loney, 1966, a familiar sight on the Falls Road.

BILL KIRK

Contents

ACKNOWLEDGEMENTS

Brian Barton; Bass Packaging; BBC Northern Ireland; Belfast Central Library; Belfast Central
Mission; Belfast City Council; Belfast Exposed; *Belfast Telegraph*; Kathleen Bell; the Bell family;
Bombardier Aerospace; Campbell College; Anne Clarke; Richard Clarke; Consarc Design Group;
Esler Crawford; Ernie Cromie; Dean of Belfast; Department of the Environment for Northern
Ireland: Monuments and Buildings Record Office; Department of the Environment for Northern
Ireland: Roads Division; Down and Connor Diocesan Archives; Ronnie Duncan; Eason and Son
Northern Ireland; Clarke Frampton; Louis Fredlander; Terry Gibbons; Robin Gordon; Clive
Graham; Keith Haines; Betty Hamilton; Gerry Healey; Fred Heatley; Austin Hunter; Imperial War
Museum; *Irish News*; *Irish Press*; Professor Narinder Kapur; Bill Kirk; Lagan College; Philip Lantin;
Helen Lewis; Linen Hall Library; Walter McAuley; McCaw, Stevenson and Orr; David
McCormack; Sean McKernan; Kenneth McNally; Claire McVeigh; Jimmy McWade; Joe
McWilliams; Mater Infirmorum Hospital; Monitor Press; John Moore; Yvonne Murphy; National
Library of Ireland; National Museums and Galleries of Northern Ireland: Ulster Folk and Transport
Museum; National Museums and Galleries of Northern Ireland: Ulster Museum; Northern Ireland
Council for Ethnic Minorities; Northern Ireland Housing Executive; O'Donovan Rossa Gaelic
Athletic Club; Odyssey Project Team; Father George O'Hanlon; PA News; Pacemaker; Olive and
George Parker; Parliament Buildings, Stormont; Victor Patterson Archive; Marcus Patton; George
Platt; Public Record Office of Northern Ireland; Queen's University Belfast; Royal Belfast Hospital
for Sick Children; Royal Victoria Hospital; St Mary's College; Salvation Army, Ireland Division;
Robert Scott; Lawrence Shivers; Norma Simon; Derek Speirs/Report; David Spence; Barry
Stewart; Stranmillis University College Library; John Todd; Ulster Aviation Society; Ulster Bank;
Diana Urquart; Eleanor Watt; Jack Woods.

Every effort has been made to trace and contact copyright holders before publication. If notified
the publishers will rectify any errors or omissions at the earliest opportunity.

LIST OF ABBREVIATIONS

BBC NI	BBC Northern Ireland
GAC	Gaelic Athletic Club
MSO	McCaw, Stevenson and Orr
NICEM	Northern Ireland Council for Ethnic Minorities
NMGNI	National Museums and Galleries of Northern Ireland
PRONI	Public Record Office of Northern Ireland
UFTM	Ulster Folk and Transport Museum
UM	Ulster Museum

Introduction

COMING INTO BELFAST LOUGH on a cold morning in 1900, passengers on the Liverpool cross-channel vessel would have heard the rhythmic booming of the Reed Horn on East Twin Island warning of fog, thickened by smoke from hundreds of factory chimneys and the pall of countless domestic fires. Ships coming into the port were guided in by three lighthouses and eight black can buoys on the County Down side and nine red buoys on the Antrim side, all constantly lit to mark the Victoria Channel. Until this 'cut' had been made in 1849, vessels had been forced to moor at low tide three miles out in the Garmoyle Pool.

The tidal mud had been dredged from the Lagan estuary in shallow water to form Queen's Island. The forest of cranes and gantries here was the most awesome sight awaiting the visitor: alongside a dozen other vessels, the hull of the White Star *Celtic* was rising high above the stocks, even larger than *Oceanic*, the biggest ship constructed anywhere in the nineteenth century, launched here in January 1899. Opposite the shipyards stood the Harbour Office, still the city's largest public building; the board of commissioners there had long striven to maintain Belfast's position as the third most important port in the United Kingdom, only exceeded by London and Liverpool. The previous twelve years had seen the completion of the graving dock, the Musgrave Channel, the tidal York Dock, the Clarence, Alexandra and Victoria wharfs, and work had begun on the Thompson graving dock which would be the largest in the world. The harbour was especially busy in 1900 for Belfast had a pivotal supply role during this anxious phase of the South African War and no fewer than twenty-one Harland and Wolff steamers had been chartered by the War Office to sustain that distant imperial conflict.

To any visitor stepping onto the quays for the first time it would soon be apparent that Belfast was one of the most significant arteries of trade and one of the greatest industrial centres in the western world. 'No city in Ireland (if indeed any in the United Kingdom) has so rapidly developed itself from insignificance to vast importance as Belfast,' the *Belfast Directory* proclaimed in 1900. Certainly its growth had few parallels: in 1757 the population was a mere 8,549 and the town had only 1,779 habitations. The census of 1901 recorded that the number of inhabitants had reached 349,180, the increase for the years 1891 to 1901 alone being over 36 per cent. It had only been in 1888 that Belfast won official recognition as a city. Though it had been completed only in 1869, the elegant Venetian Gothic Town Hall in Victoria Street was soon considered to be too modest to be the municipal centre. The White Linen Hall in Donegall Square was demolished and on 18 October 1898 the lord lieutenant, the Earl of Cadogan, laid the foundation stone of the City Hall. The building taking shape behind the hoardings would be an expression of pride in Belfast's achievement in being the city with the world's largest shipyard, ropeworks, aerated waters factory, linen mill, tea machinery and fan-making works, handkerchief factory, spiral-guided gasometer, linen machinery works, and tobacco factory.

In their best-selling book on Ireland published in 1843, Mr and Mrs S.C. Hall had observed: 'The cleanly and bustling appearance of Belfast is decidedly un-national. That it is in Ireland but not of it is a remark ever on the lips of visitors from south or west'. Certainly Belfast had much in common with British city ports such as Liverpool, Glasgow and Newcastle-on-Tyne, but at the same time it was an Irish city with problems unique to Ireland. Such had been the influx of immigrants from the Ulster countryside in the nineteenth century that in 1901 only 39 per cent of the city's inhabitants had been born in Belfast. These incomers had brought with them unfinished business accumulated over two and a half centuries and in densely populated rows of terraced houses folk memories of conquest, massacre, confiscation, persecution and resistance remained stubbornly alive. During the home rule crisis passions raged so fiercely that by the summer of 1914 civil war threatened. Conflict at home was postponed by total war on the European mainland but, following terrible sacrifices at the Somme, Gallipoli and elsewhere, intercommunal violence erupted with unprecedented ferocity in 1920. While the fighting still raged in the streets, Belfast became the capital of the first devolved region of the United Kingdom.

Radical changes in the pattern of world trade, hastened by the world war and dislocated by the collapse in confidence following the Wall Street Crash of 1929, hit Belfast hard. For many citizens these were years of acute hardship: nevertheless, three-quarters of the work force were employed. Those who regarded Belfast as a bleak, dour and joyless city, overlooked the camaraderie of tight-knit communities and the constant exchange of teasing witticisms known as 'banter' in the mills, factories and workshops. The cinema was accessible to all and a walk or a trip on the tram brought people quickly to the open country, particularly to Bellevue, an urban recreational ground with few equals.

Belfast was almost completely unprepared when the Germans launched devastating air raids on the city in the spring of 1941. The blitz exposed for all to see the consequences of two decades of neglect as the impoverished sought refuge on the hillsides and in the countryside. Yet even while the war was still being fought, the most sustained improvement in the living standards of citizens in the twentieth century had begun. There was work for all while the shipyards, aircraft factory, mills and engineering works of Belfast strove to feed the Allied war machine and peace was not followed by the slump that so many feared. The welfare state may well have had a more beneficial impact on Belfast than on any other major city in the United Kingdom. The city did not recover its pre-eminent economic position but for individual citizens the quality of life improved immeasurably. Visitors remarked on how uninviting Belfast was on a wet Sunday but this was a lively city with citizens determined to enjoy themselves, joining long queues for the Ritz, the Empire or the Saturday matinée at dozens of picture houses, and dancing indefatigably at the Plaza and the Floral Hall.

So prevalent was the calm of the post-war decades that many, not only in America and on the Continent but also in Britain, would have had difficulty in locating Belfast on a map. The explosion of intercommunal conflict in the summer of 1969 changed that and, as Belfast became the most violent city in western Europe, districts such as the Shankill, Ardoyne, the

The Floral Hall at Bellevue, mid-1940s, an extremely popular venue for dances.
BELFAST CITY COUNCIL

Falls, Tiger's Bay, the New Lodge and Short Strand became familiar across the world. Around half of those killed and maimed over quarter of a century were in the Greater Belfast area; bombs destroyed many of the city's most venerable landmarks as well as lives and jobs; much of the city resembled a battle zone; and for years darkness brought terror to whole districts. Even while the violence still periodically dislocated much of the city, however, the regeneration of Belfast had begun: some of the worst slums in the United Kingdom were replaced by well-designed dwellings in the Markets, Donegall Pass, Sandy Row, the lower Falls, the Newtownards Road and elsewhere under the direction of the Northern Ireland Housing Executive; gaps and scars left by bombs and decay were filled by new department stores, office blocks and public buildings; and surviving buildings from the Victorian era, such as the Custom House and the McCausland building, were cleaned of their grime and completely refurbished. Even in the worst periods of violence, the King's Hall, for example, attracted capacity audiences to see entertainers of international repute. From the early 1980s restaurants, cafes, clubs, hot-food bars and fashionable pubs opened in the city – particularly in the 'Golden Mile' around Shaftesbury Square, the Dublin Road and along Great Victoria Street and Bedford Street – drawing people in for entertainment and relaxation on an unprecedented scale. 'The spirit of the Blitz has been institutionalised so that people preserve and protect what bits of normality remain to them,' Patrick Bishop wrote in the *Observer* in 1984. 'There is something brave and encouraging about the indefatigable diners and the denizens of the discos.'

In the years of rapid growth Belfast had produced talented engineers, scientists and

The Laganside development, 1999. In the foreground is the Lagan Weir and Lookout and further upstream on the right, beyond the Queen's Bridge and the Albert Bridge, are the Waterfront Hall, the Hilton Hotel, and the British Telecom Tower. Fashionable and attractive riverside apartments can be seen on the left.

ESLER CRAWFORD

craftsmen, but few writers and artists of note. From the beginning of the twentieth century the international reputation won by the painter Sir John Lavery seemed to mark a quickening of the city's cultural life. Between the wars Louis MacNeice emerged as one of the finest poets writing in English but it was in the 1960s that a remarkable renaissance got under way, led by poets such as Michael Longley, John Hewitt and Derek Mahon, and novelist Brian Moore. Musicians and singers, such as Van Morrison, Heather Harper, James Galway and Barry Douglas, also drew the world's attention to their native city. That revival, cutting across the sectarian divide and partly generated by the beneficial impact of the 1947 Education Act, continued and blossomed to the extent that as the century was drawing to a close no one spoke disparagingly any more of the city as a cultural wasteland.

At the end of the century, after several false starts, Belfast began to enjoy peace at a level never before experienced by citizens of thirty years and younger. The city looked brighter and cleaner than it had ever done and nowhere was this transformation more apparent than along the Lagan, freshly adorned with the Waterfront Hall, the Dargan Bridge, the refurbished Clarendon Dock, fashionable apartments, offices, hotels and restaurants, and attractively lit walkways, and with ambitious developments at Cromac Wood and below the Queen's Bridge. Acute problems remained but citizens seemed to be more determined in their search for an accommodation of clashing aspirations. As the millennium drew to a close the people of Belfast were showing an obvious faith in the future of their city and a growing conviction that it could richly sustain them and their children for many decades to come.

JONATHAN BARDON
BELFAST
OCTOBER 1999

1900s

OPPOSITE:
Decorated with bunting for the royal visit of King Edward VII and Queen Alexandra in July 1903, the half-built City Hall rises from the grounds of the White Linen Hall, demolished in 1896. The great quadrangle and portico of Portland stone is almost completed and the statue of Queen Victoria is already in place.
LINEN HALL LIBRARY

The new sewerage system installed under the provisions of the Belfast Main Drainage Act of 1887 failed to prevent the flooding of Donegall Square in 1901, caused by heavy rain and a high tide.
PRONI

AT THE BEGINNING OF THE TWENTIETH CENTURY the chief point of interest in Belfast was a massive construction project in the city centre. The Old Town Hall in Victoria Street had long been regarded as too modest a municipal centre for Belfast, which was now the largest city in Ireland and the twelfth biggest in the United Kingdom. From 1896 demolition work had begun on the late-eighteenth-century White Linen Hall and in its place the City Hall was taking shape. The winner of the competition to select the design of the city's new administrative centre was a young London architect, Alfred Brumwell Thomas. Built by H. and J. Martin, the City Hall cost £360,000, twice the original estimate, causing the Local Government Board at Dublin Castle to order a special inquiry. Opened in 1906, this flamboyant Portland stone building, with a rich Italian marble interior and a dome 173 feet high, was a reflection of Belfast's commercial and industrial success and the confidence of the corporation in the city's future. The same confidence was shown in the extensive rebuilding of Donegall Square – including the erection of the massive sandstone Scottish Provident Institution, the Northern Bank, the tall Ocean Buildings and the Scottish Temperance Buildings – to make it the hub of a great modern city.

Belfast continued to grow, but at a slower rate than in the previous century: its population rose from 349,180 in 1901 to 386,947 in 1911. In part this was due to a slowdown in the building of houses for skilled and unskilled workers, who were finding it more difficult to pay the rents of between four and six shillings asked for the kitchen and parlour terraced houses so characteristic of these years. Food prices rose by 29 per cent between 1895 and 1912 without a corresponding increase in wage levels. Twenty-six per cent of the male work force was skilled, earning on average around forty shillings a week. Few Catholics were included in this aristocracy of labour, though there were as many Protestants as Catholics in the unskilled labour force. Catholics tended to live in the more dilapidated houses, some of which were razed in the Millfield area, and only one Catholic household in sixteen had a fixed bath, compared with one in six in Protestant households. Inflation increased the distress of the working class and these years saw the growth of a militant labour movement and the most tenacious strike Ireland had yet seen, the Belfast dock strike of 1907.

Belfast's city boundary had been extended in 1896 and this period witnessed the building of middle-class suburbs such as Rosetta, Bloomfield, the Glen Road, and between the Antrim and Shore roads, though Sir Robert McConnell's Cliftonville Garden Colony proved to be an over-ambitious project. Suburban development was assisted by the extension of the tramways, taken over by the corporation in 1904 and electrified at the cost of a million pounds by 1905. The final departure of the middle classes to the outskirts left the city centre dominated by commercial premises; public buildings such as the Municipal Technical Institute opened in 1907, and places of entertainment including the splendid Grand Opera House, completed in 1895 and briefly renamed the Palace of Varieties between 1904 and 1909.

The end of the Boer War caused a slump in orders for the city's industrial concerns and during the recession of 1904–5 nearly one-fifth of shipyard workers were unemployed. Workman Clark, the 'wee yard', nevertheless remained a leading builder of vessels for carrying fruit and refrigerated meat. Lord Pirrie, chairman of Harland and Wolff, allowed ships to be built at a loss while he organised a massive programme of modernisation, putting the firm in readiness for an upturn in demand in 1910.

OPPOSITE TOP:

A steam tug pulls a lighter on the Lagan close to Queen's Quay in 1903. Belfast was by far the busiest port in Ireland and depended for its prosperity on the export of linen, engineering products, aerated waters, rope and cordage, tobacco and tea machinery. The city's industries, gasworks and domestic hearths were completely dependent on English and Scottish coal, most of it brought ashore at Queen's Quay.

NMGNI UM

OPPOSITE BOTTOM:

The barge *Shamrock*, with Attie and James Mullan on board, being drawn along the Lagan at Drumbridge, with Johnny Douglas leading the horse. Built to extend to Lisburn by 1765 and to Lough Neagh by the 1790s, the Lagan Canal competed more successfully with railways than with other Irish canals.

NMGNI UM

BELOW:

Launched by Harland and Wolff from number 2 slip, north yard, on 4 April 1901, *Celtic* was the largest man-made moving object ever built in the world up to that time. Wooden blocks and other debris are being recovered from the water while tugs prepare to take the liner to its fitting-out wharf. The ways in the foreground are about to be smeared with soft soap and tallow in preparation for laying the keel of the next ship.

NMGNI UM

RIGHT:

At the beginning of the century children in Belfast faced the perils of poverty, poor sanitation and disease. The Citizens' Association was so concerned about the state of the city's health that it persuaded the government to set up the Vice-Regal Commission of Inquiry in 1906. The report published in 1908 found the death rate was around the same as in Liverpool and Manchester but the death rate from typhoid was the highest for any city and that the tuberculosis rate was higher than in Dublin. Clean water flowing by gravity down forty miles of pipes from the Mournes from 1901 onwards brought much improvement, and vigorous action by the first medical officer of health, Dr H.W. Baillie, almost removed typhoid as a threat by 1911.

BELFAST CENTRAL MISSION

BELOW:

The Custom House Steps, 1901: the most popular venue for open-air speakers, the Custom House is being used on this occasion by the Belfast Central Mission, set up by the Methodists in 1889. These services were held every Sunday afternoon right up to the 1970s. At other times the steps formed Belfast's equivalent of Speakers' Corner.

BELFAST CENTRAL MISSION

Jim Larkin addressing dockers by the quays during the Belfast dock strike of 1907. Larkin had come from Liverpool at the beginning of the year to organise a branch of the National Union of Dock Labourers. He soon united the Protestant cross-channel and Catholic deep-sea dockers by his charismatic leadership and powerful oratory – 'Half a dozen words from Jim Larkin and you were all together,' one trade union member recalled. The strike began on 9 May when dockers who had been agitating for better conditions found themselves locked out by their employers and their places taken by drafts of imported blacklegs.

BELFAST CENTRAL LIBRARY

BELOW:

Motor vans delivering under police escort at the *Belfast Evening Telegraph* offices on Royal Avenue during the 1907 dock strike. By the beginning of July iron moulders, coal heavers and carters had joined the dockers, bringing economic life in the city close to paralysis. When the police mutinied, the government sent warships into Belfast Lough and cavalry and foot soldiers onto the streets. The strikers drifted back to work in stages during the remaining months of the year with almost nothing gained.

BELFAST CENTRAL LIBRARY

ABOVE:
The Royal Victoria Hospital, previously the Frederick Street Hospital, was formally opened by Edward VII on 27 July 1903. This photograph, taken about 1905, gives a view from the Grosvenor Road before the Musgrave Wing was built. The gate lodge and the boiler-house chimney behind it can be seen on the left.

ROYAL VICTORIA HOSPITAL

Interior of the Mater Infirmorum Hospital in 1900. A branch of the Sisters of Mercy set up in St Paul's Convent in 1867 and in 1883 Bishop Patrick Dorrian, of the diocese of Down and Connor, bought Bedeque House on the Crumlin Road for use as a dispensary and a hospital with thirty-four beds. Clinical teaching of medical students began there in October 1908.

MATER INFIRMORUM HOSPITAL

Peter's Hill

Abbey Street

Abbey Street, a wretched alley off Peter's Hill. Despite all the glitter and ostentation of the Edwardian era, the working people of Belfast, in common with those in other major cities in the United Kingdom, suffered a severe drop in living standards as a result of inflation. This decline was graphically shown by the sharp fall in the number of new houses built to be rented by the working classes: between 1901 and 1911 Belfast's housing stock only increased by 3.16 per cent. This street was to benefit from a limited slum-clearance scheme just before the First World War but, as the gap between rich and poor yawned wide, developers concentrated on houses for the middle classes, notably at Cliftonville, Fortwilliam, Rosetta, Ravenhill, Cregagh, Knock, Belmont and Balmoral.

Men working in a labour yard self-help
scheme set up in Glengall Street in 1904.
Though this was a decade of impressive
growth overall, there were alarming
fluctuations from year to year. A severe
recession in the winter of 1904–5 left 19 per
cent of shipyard workers unemployed. The
only safety nets for the unemployed were
the workhouse on the Lisburn Road and
schemes such as this one sponsored by
Church organisations. Old age pensions
were not introduced until 1908 and
contributory National Insurance
schemes began in 1911.

BELFAST CENTRAL MISSION

BELOW:
Mill girls, York Street Flax Spinning Mill.
The manufacture of linen by powered
machinery began in Belfast in the 1820s and
developed rapidly when the cotton fields
were devastated during the American Civil
War. By the end of the 1860s Belfast had
become the world centre of the linen
industry and retained that position during
the first decades of the twentieth century.
Up to the 1950s more than half the people
at work in the city were employed in this
industry. Wages were lower than in any other
textile industry and fine flax dust, known as
'pouce', and high levels of humidity posed
constant hazards to health.

LINEN HALL LIBRARY

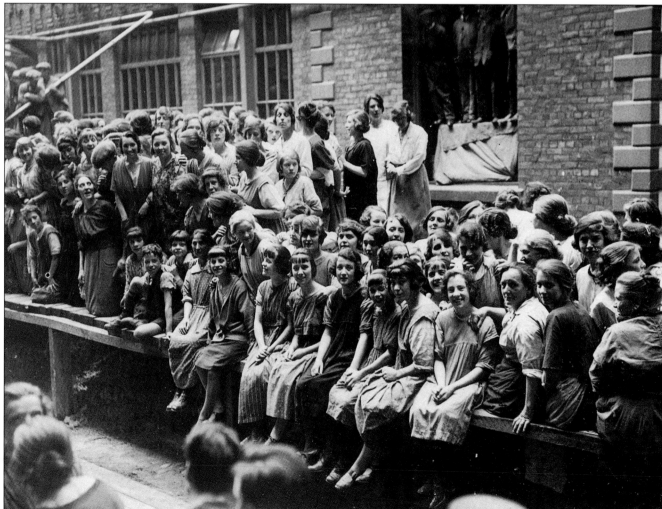

LEFT:
Young women binding and packing at Loopbridge on the Castlereagh Road, the main premises of McCaw, Stevenson and Orr, Ireland's largest firm of printers, lithographers and publishers. Incorporating in 1901 the business of Marcus Ward and Company, inventors of the mass-produced, coloured Christmas card, this firm specialised in printing boxes for the Meccano Company of Liverpool and 'glacier' transparent window decoration.

MSO

BELOW:
Lithography artists at McCaw, Stevenson and Orr. Artwork had to be painstakingly copied directly onto stone before the printing process.

MSO

RIGHT:
Members of the 30th Boys'
Brigade Company, Grosvenor
Road, in the Botanic Gardens.
The acquisition of the
Botanic Gardens in 1893 by
the corporation, previously
confined to members, was of
great benefit to a city rather
short of urban parks.

BELFAST CENTRAL MISSION

BELOW:
The boathouse at Stranmillis.
The Lagan Canal was
navigable from the sea to
Stranmillis, where the first of
twenty-seven locks was
located, and it was here that
the Belfast Boat Club
established its headquarters.
This was the fabled site of
Molly Ward's tavern, where in
the 1790s United Irishmen
plotted revolution.

LINEN HALL LIBRARY

VE HILL. BELFAST. 9869. W. L.

LEFT:
Cave Hill, previously named Ben Madigan. In his *Thorough Guide Series: Ireland, 1902*, M.J.B. Baddeley recommended ascending by a path 'at first railed and paled, and bristling with trespass boards' to this 'bulwark of almost perpendicular basaltic rock, from which there is a fine bird's-eye view of the country south and east, not improved by the smoke of Belfast'. It was said that insurgents who survived the Battle of Antrim in 1798 took refuge in these caves.

NATIONAL LIBRARY OF IRELAND

BELOW:
Belfast Castle on the slopes of Cave Hill. Built to a design by W. J. Barre in 1867, this was still the private residence of the 9th Earl of Shaftesbury, whose mother had inherited what was left of the Donegall estates in 1883. The earl took part in municipal politics, being elected lord mayor of Belfast in 1907. He gave the castle and its grounds to the city in 1934.

NMGNI UM

The Palace and the Hippodrome, Great Victoria Street. In December 1895 Belfast acquired a splendid Grand Opera House, designed by Frank Matcham, with a lavish oriental-style interior. Shortly afterwards the Hippodrome opened its doors and, possibly because its programmes were so popular, the Opera House changed its name to the Palace of Varieties in 1904. Eventually the Hippodrome concentrated on music hall entertainment and built up audiences for silent films, while the Grand Opera House – as it became again in 1909 – attracted to its stage such celebrated performers as Sarah Bernhardt, Beerbohm Tree and Johnston Forbes-Robertson.

LEFT:
The Alhambra Theatre, North Street. Founded by actor–manager Dan Lowrey in 1873, it was for long Belfast's most popular music hall. From 1896 films were shown, making it one of Belfast's first picture houses.

NATIONAL LIBRARY OF IRELAND

OPPOSITE BOTTOM:
The laying of track for electric trams at the junction of York Street, Royal Avenue and Donegall Street in 1905. The Belfast Street Tramway Company was bought over by the corporation in 1904 and converted to electric traction by the end of the following year. Previously too expensive for most citizens, by 1906 the trams sold 30 million trips in a year.

NMGNI UM

LEFT:
The Grosvenor Hall, Grosvenor Road, had been erected in just three months by Musgrave Brothers, a Belfast firm with an international reputation for their patent stable and house fittings, supplying such people of title and wealth as Krupps of Essen, the Prince of Wales, Monsieur Eiffel and the Khedive of Egypt. Opened in 1895 by Belfast Central Mission, the hall organised 'Happy Evenings', including slide shows featuring A.R. Hogg's screen and gas projector.

BELFAST CENTRAL MISSION

16

RIGHT:
Interior of the Belfast Museum in College Square North. A three-storey stucco Greek revival terraced house, it was built in 1831 for the Belfast Natural History and Philosophical Society, founded in 1821. Named the Belfast Museum in 1901, it moved to become part of the Belfast Museum and Art Gallery at Stranmillis in 1929. Its former home is now the Old Museum Arts Centre.

LINEN HALL LIBRARY

BELOW:
Following the demolition of the White Linen Hall in 1896, the library of the Belfast Society for Promoting Knowledge had to move across the road to a former linen warehouse in Donegall Square North, where it remains to this day as Ireland's only subscribing library. This photograph shows that the Linen Hall Library, as it is now known, has retained its character and ambience.

LINEN HALL LIBRARY

The Christian Brothers Schools in Barrack Street. This teaching order had been invited to set up in Belfast by Dr Patrick Dorrian, Catholic bishop of Down and Connor, in 1870. Barrack Street was one of two Christian Brothers secondary schools in the city and together they educated three times as many pupils as the diocesan seminary, St Malachy's College. There is no doubt that the Brothers provided secondary educational opportunities to many poorer Catholics and it was largely due to them that by 1914 Catholic schools educated 468 pupils at secondary level, that is, 23 per cent of those receiving a 'superior' education in the city, which represented parity with the Catholic proportion of the city's population as a whole.

BELFAST CITY COUNCIL

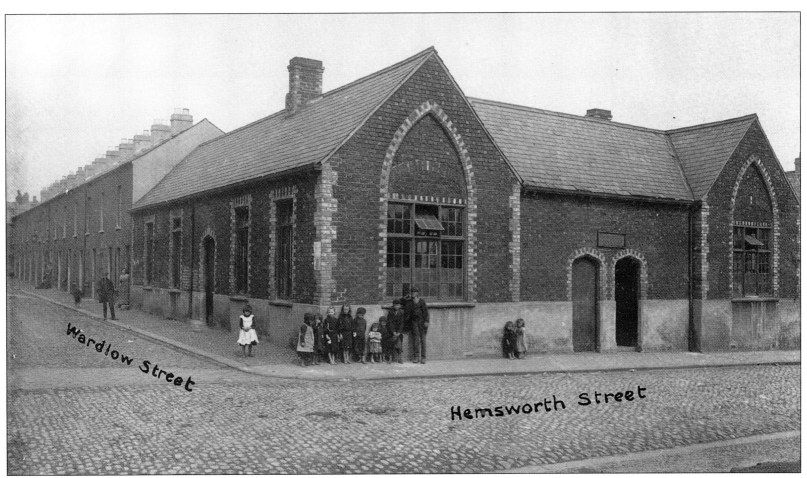

Hemsworth Street National School, the Shankill, 1912. For the great majority in the city schooling went no further than elementary education. National schools had been set up in 1831 and, despite early attempts to make them nondenominational, soon came under the management of the Churches. Though Belfast was the most literate corner in Ireland, by the beginning of the century the city's schools were seriously under-funded and unable to take all applicants despite legislation in 1892 making attendance compulsory.

BELFAST CITY COUNCIL

RIGHT:
Oswald's on the Shankill Road, displaying local and imported fruit and vegetables, with bunches of bananas well to the fore. Workman Clark, known as the 'wee yard' though it was the sixth largest shipbuilder in the United Kingdom, pioneered the construction of refrigerated vessels for carrying bananas for the United Fruit Company of Boston, and Elders and Fyffes.

ELEANOR WATT

BELOW:
Carlisle Circus looking down Clifton Street towards the city centre. Right foreground: statue of the Reverend Hugh 'Roaring' Hanna, a noted controversialist; to the right of the statue (blown up in the 1970s): the Carlisle Memorial Methodist Church; on the left: Hanna's Presbyterian church, St Enoch's; on the right-hand side of Clifton Street: the Belfast headquarters of the Orange Order topped with a bronze equestrian statue of William of Orange, weighing seven tons.

LINEN HALL LIBRARY

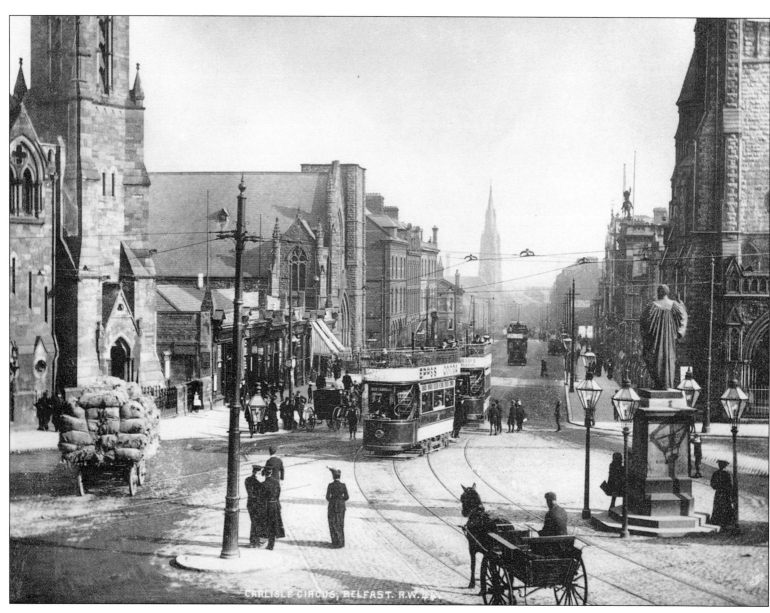

1910s

An excursion setting out for Bangor, organised by the Belfast Central Mission. The mission in these years was particularly concerned about 'waif' children from Belfast's poorest areas. In 1912 it was revealed that around 450 families in the city were each living in one room despite the fact that in Belfast there were over 10,000 empty houses. In the same year it was shown that school attendance in the city was only 76 per cent – in other words, 24 out of every 100 children were on the loose every day.

BELFAST CENTRAL MISSION

RIGHT:
Children from the inner city crossing the Queen's Bridge on an annual excursion to Bangor. The Queen's Bridge had been erected in 1843 to replace the Long Bridge, which had been the longest bridge in both Ireland and Britain. The bridge was the busiest in the city, witnessing great armies of shipyard workers crossing it every morning and evening.

BELFAST CENTRAL MISSION

BELOW:
The Queen's Quay terminal of the Belfast and County Down Railway shortly after it had been rebuilt in 1912.

NMGNI UM

ON 20 OCTOBER 1910 *Olympic*, the world's biggest ship, which for two years had towered 228 feet above the slips on Queen's Island in a huge gantry, was launched by Harland and Wolff in a blaze of publicity. On 31 May 1911 fitting-out was complete and the great liner steamed out of Belfast Lough. A few hours earlier *Titanic*, 1,000 gross tons heavier than her sister ship, had left the ways. The tragic loss of *Titanic* during her maiden voyage on 15 April 1912, with almost 1,500 passengers and crew, cast a shadow over the reputation of the Belfast yard though it was not until the 1920s that Harland and Wolff faced economic difficulties.

Another dark cloud hung over Belfast in these years. The two general elections of 1910 left the Irish Parliamentary Party holding the balance of power at Westminster; home rule seemed imminent, and passions ran high as unionists made Belfast the pivot of their campaign against the establishment of Dublin rule. Then in 1914, as Ireland teetered on the brink of civil conflict, the First World War began. Protected from attack by the Royal Navy and out of range of German zeppelins, the shipyards, mills and engineering shops of Belfast strove to meet the seemingly insatiable demands of the British war economy. The young men of the city, however, made a heavy sacrifice in blood, particularly at the Somme on 1 July 1916. The war failed to dilute the deep communal divisions and opposing political aspirations of citizens and the 1918 election revealed a population more polarised than ever. As the decade closed, Belfast began plunging into the worst violence witnessed for more than a century.

OPPOSITE TOP:
Belfast Celtic, winners of the Gold Cup for the 1911–12 season, after beating
Glentoran 2–0 in the final. Formed in 1891 to 'imitate their Scottish
counterparts in style, play and charity', the team was accepted into the Senior
League in 1896 and acquired Celtic Park on the Falls Road in 1901.

BELFAST TELEGRAPH

BELOW:
The *Titanic* in the channel of Belfast Lough on 2 April 1912. The tugs
Huskisson and *Herculaneum* are escorting the liner astern while *Hornby* and
Herald keep her steady ahead. Thirteen days later *Titanic* sank in
the north-west Atlantic with the loss of nearly 1,500 lives.

NMGNI UFTM

O'Donovan Rossa GAA club, in 1916. In that year the Irish Republican Brotherhood, headed by the Belfast piano tuner Denis McCullough, planned an insurrection with German help. Militants from Cork came north to help co-ordinate the rising there, but due mainly to a breakdown in communications, the signal came too late to Belfast and the rebellion was largely confined to Dublin during Easter week. The Munster men stayed for a time and founded the GAA club on the Falls Road, named after the Cork Fenian, Jeremiah O'Donovan Rossa. Many of these men became active in the IRA from 1919 to 1920 and one of them, Joe McKelvey of Belfast, joined the Irregulars during the 1922–3 civil war and was executed in reprisal by the Free State government in December 1922.

O'DONOVAN ROSSA GAC

By the beginning of 1912 Herbert Asquith's Liberal government depended on the support of the Irish Parliamentary Party to stay in power, and home rule for Ireland was promised. The Ulster Liberal Association, represented by Lord Pirrie, chairman of Harland and Wolff, organised a demonstration at the Celtic Park football grounds on 8 February after the corporation had denied it the use of the Ulster Hall. The main speakers were John Redmond, leader of the Nationalists, and Winston Churchill, the British home secretary charged with the responsibility of introducing the Home Rule Bill. On the way to the meeting Churchill was jostled in a motor car by hostile unionists, many of whom would have been Harland and Wolff shipyard workers.

PRONI

ULSTER LIBERAL ASSOCIATION.

The Right Hon. LORD PIRRIE, K.P., H.M.L.

The Right Hon. WINSTON CHURCHILL, M.P.

Mr. JOHN REDMOND, M.P.

Unreserved 1/-

CELTIC PARK FOOTBALL GROUNDS, FEBRUARY 8th, 1912.

Meeting at 1 o'clock.   Doors open at 12 o'clock.

GRAND STAND

The 1912 home rule meeting was held in a great marquee in Celtic Park, which was just as well as there were heavy downpours that afternoon. In the densely packed tent pickpockets had a field day: three Royal Irish Constabulary policemen are showing some of the many empty purses and wallets found the morning after the meeting.

NMGNI UM

LEFT:

Sir Edward Carson, leader of the Ulster Unionists since February 1910. At Strandtown in 1911 he warned: 'We must be prepared, the morning Home Rule passes, ourselves to become responsible for the government of the Protestant Province of Ulster.'

PRONI

BELOW:

Andrew Bonar Law, leader of the Conservative Party, surrounded by supporters in Royal Avenue, after his speech at the Unionist demonstration against home rule at Balmoral on Easter Tuesday 1912. 'Once again you hold the pass, the pass for the Empire,' he had said. 'You are a besieged city. The timid have left you; your Lundies have betrayed you; but you have closed your gates.' His father had been a Presbyterian minister in Coleraine and he felt a close bond with Ulster Protestants opposed to the establishment of a parliament in Dublin. By publicly committing his party to the Ulster Unionist Council's campaign he helped to precipitate the greatest constitutional crisis yet witnessed in the United Kingdom.

BELFAST CENTRAL MISSION

RIGHT:
Sir Edward Carson was the first to sign the Solemn League and Covenant, placed on a Union flag draped over a table directly under the dome of the City Hall on Ulster Day, Saturday 28 September 1912. On his left is Captain James Craig, Unionist MP for East Down, who masterminded this climax to the campaign against the third Home Rule Bill and later became prime minister of Northern Ireland.

NMGNI UM

BELOW:
Donegall Square, 28 September 1912. As Carson and other leading Unionist dignitaries put their signatures to the covenant in the City Hall, bowler-hatted stewards held back a huge crowd; they re-emerged to tempestuous cheering. Then the stewards struggled to regulate the flow of men eager to sign. A double row of desks stretching right round the building made it possible for 550 to sign simultaneously.

Reporting for the *Pall Mall Gazette*, J.L. Garvin wrote: 'Seen from the topmost outside gallery of the dome, the square below and the streets striking away from it were black with people. Through all the mass, with drums and fifes, the clubs marched all day.'

BBC NI

LEFT:
Unionists and Conservatives were opposed to giving votes to women and therefore only men were entitled to sign the covenant. Women, however, signed their own declaration as this photograph shows. Altogether 471,414 men and women who could prove Ulster birth signed either the covenant or the declaration, over 30,000 more women, in fact, than men.

BELFAST CENTRAL LIBRARY

OPPOSITE TOP:
Men of the Ulster Volunteer Force at Craigavon, Captain James Craig's home at Strandtown in east Belfast; the UVF was formed in early 1913. While the authorities were deflected by a decoy ship in Belfast Lough, the UVF brought in 216 tons of arms from Hamburg at Larne, Bangor and Donaghadee on the night of 19–20 April 1914. Although the government rushed troops to Ulster and sent warships into Belfast Lough, it subsequently decided against attempting to disarm the loyalists.

BELFAST CENTRAL LIBRARY

ABOVE:
Senior pupils from Campbell College, Belmont, at an Officers' Training Corps camp in England in 1913. Since the life expectancy of British officers on the Western Front was only around three weeks, those who joined up would have been very fortunate to have survived the war.

ROBIN GORDON

RIGHT:
Dorothy Evans (marked with an X) and Madge Muir appearing at the Belfast Summons Court on 22 April 1914. They had been released from prison a week earlier after going on hunger strike and were due to appear at the police court on 20 April – instead they drove defiantly through the city centre in a motor car decked out with suffragist flags, circling the courts several times, and were rearrested soon afterwards. No male politician of any standing in Ireland championed their cause.

BELFAST TELEGRAPH

BELOW:
The 36th (Ulster) Division's final parade in front of the City Hall on 8 May 1915 before setting out for the front. When the First World War broke out Ireland seemed on the brink of civil conflict, particularly in Belfast where the UVF and the Irish Volunteers were parading in adjacent streets. Both sets of armed men then pledged themselves to the Allied cause. The UVF were allowed to stay together in the 36th Division. This photograph shows ambulances which had been paid for by collections made all over Ulster.

PRONI

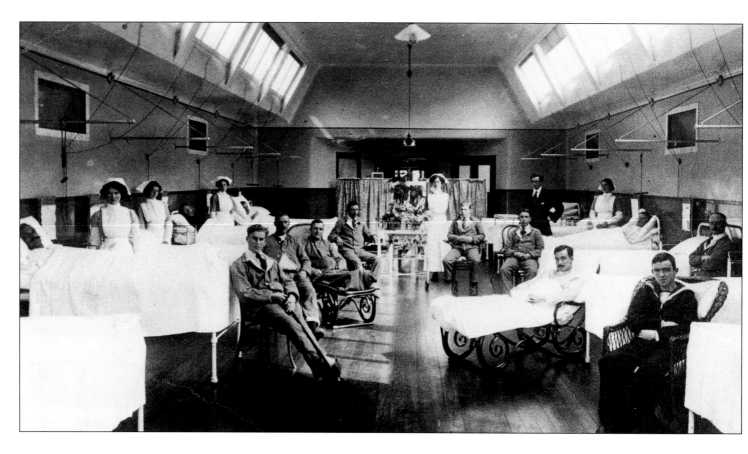

Men playing quoits at the temporary UVF hospital at Queen's University. The biggest battle the world had yet seen began on 1 July 1916 at the Somme, after a six-day Allied artillery barrage. The massive bombardment had neither cut the wire nor knocked out the enemy machine-gun nests and the result was that the advancing men were slaughtered during a day when the British Army suffered the greatest loss in its history. On 12 July there were no Orange parades in Belfast: when the clocks struck noon all work was suspended, trams stopped in their tracks and trains pulled up as citizens remembered the fallen in deep silence.

OPPOSITE TOP:

Soldiers recovering from their wounds in the Royal Victoria Hospital, 1915. The *Irish News* had reported that as early as 5 August 1914 'about six hundred men attached to the Irish Volunteers in Belfast were called up, and there was a great gathering to wish them God-speed . . . while at the same time a quota of the Ulster Volunteers was being "seen off"' by a cheering crowd with a band and pipers'.

ROYAL VICTORIA HOSPITAL

BELOW:

High Street on Peace Day, 28 June 1919. Almost nine months after the armistice, the Germans signed the Treaty of Versailles, and in Belfast there were anxieties whether or not celebration was justified, but the trams were decorated and flags and bunting were decked out in any case.

NMGNI UM

Hughes's Mill, where Divis Street and the Falls Road meet. The founder, Bernard Hughes, was Belfast's first notable Catholic businessman and the first Catholic councillor, elected as a Liberal in 1855. He is remembered in a well-known skipping rhyme:

Barney Hughes's bread,
Sticks to your belly like lead,
Not a bit of wonder,
You fart like thunder,
Barney Hughes's bread.

The Methodist church in the foreground shows that the area had a Protestant population early in the century and Protestant churches there still had active congregations right up to the late 1960s.

NMGNI UFTM

Offices of the Society of St Vincent de Paul in Millfield. Founded in Paris in 1833, the society was brought to Ireland in 1844 and its first conference was formed in Belfast at St Mary's in Chapel Lane in 1850. The organisation strove to put the gospel into practice by working to relieve the distress of the poor. It provided vital help to down-and-outs and the destitute, who were denied assistance under the Poor Law, and in Belfast it played a leading role in founding the first Catholic schools. Many of its records and books, which it lent out freely to the poor, were lost when the Ulster Special Constabulary occupied St Mary's Hall in the 1920s.

BELFAST CITY COUNCIL

LEFT:
The Catholic Repository on the corner of Mill Street and Queen Street. The census of 1861 showed that 34 per cent of Belfast's population was Catholic, but while numbers continued to rise as the city grew, the percentage had fallen to 23 per cent by the 1920s. This change was largely accounted for by Catholic adult male out-migration, supplemented by a new teenage exodus.

BELFAST CITY COUNCIL

BELOW:
Cromac Square, created around 1890 by the demolition of a block of houses between Cromac Street and Market Street. Stone's bicycle shop at numbers 6–10 was the inspiration for *Spokesong*, Stewart Parker's first play. The square was on the main route through the Markets, probably the first Catholic enclave in Belfast.

BELFAST CITY COUNCIL

Barrack Court in the Millfield area just before demolition.
Two families often lived in these tiny four-roomed dwellings and in such
cramped conditions diseases such as tuberculosis flourished.

St Matthew's Schools on the Shankill Road with the filthy Glenwood river flowing alongside it in 1915. Charles S.H. Vane-Tempest-Stewart, the 7th Marquess of Londonderry, was Northern Ireland's first minister of education and he was determined to improve the deplorable condition of the region's elementary schools as revealed in the Lynn report in 1922. His attempts to make the schools nondenominational were fiercely opposed by both the Protestant and Catholic Churches.

BELFAST CITY COUNCIL

The Great Northern Railway line close to the Lisburn Road at
Tate's Avenue, a Protestant working-class district of kitchen and
parlour houses. The marshy ground at the end of Tate's Avenue
discouraged builders and was known as the Bog Meadows, an
urban haven for herons, reed warblers and kestrels.

The Lisburn Road at the eastern end of the avenue has been
described as a 'social canyon', with comfortable and spacious
middle-class villas on the other side of the road extending to
the exclusive Malone Road.

BELFAST CITY COUNCIL

1920s

VISITORS TO BELFAST IN THE NINETEENTH CENTURY had often observed that it looked more like an English or a Scottish city rather than an Irish one. But it was an Irish city and the problems of Ireland were to be seen there in a concentrated, virulent form. As the island's political future was being decided in the 1918 general election and during the Anglo-Irish War (1919–21), and by the 1920 Government of Ireland Act and the 1921 Anglo-Irish Treaty, much of Belfast was convulsed by intercommunal warfare more intense than all the nineteenth-century sectarian riots put together. The price in blood was heavy: between July 1920 and July 1922 the civilian death toll was 416, of which 257 were Catholics, who formed only a quarter of the city's population. In 1921 Ireland was partitioned and Belfast became the capital of the United Kingdom's first devolved region.

The problems facing Belfast from religious and cultural divisions might have been more easily managed had the city continued to enjoy the economic buoyancy of the pre-war years. The severe slump which set in during the winter of 1920 was no temporary downswing: Belfast's limited range of specialised export industries faced competition from new centres of production overseas and suffered from over-production and dislocation arising from the war. By January 1922, 27 per cent of insured workers in the city were out of work and for the rest of the decade around one-fifth were unemployed. Political turmoil not only discouraged fresh investment but also had a baleful effect on the Catholic minority: relief organisations estimated that between 8,700 and 11,000 Catholics had been driven from their employment in 1920–2.

The first proportional representation elections anywhere in the United Kingdom were held for the Belfast Corporation in 1920 and the broad range of councillors elected stimulated lively municipal debates. The abolition of PR by the Northern Ireland government in 1922 had a stultifying effect and the corporation lost the innovative drive it had shown before the war. Unlike large cities on the other side of the Irish Sea, Belfast's efforts to build homes for heroes were pitiful: only 2,600 houses were built by the corporation between the wars, most of them in the 1920s. In contrast, cultural life in Belfast showed signs of revival and development.

Sectarian rioting at the corner of York Street and Donegall Street in 1920, with the Grand Metropolitan Hotel in the foreground. In that year the political future of the island hung in the balance as a cabinet committee at Westminster worked out the details of the Government of Ireland Bill and Dáil Éireann recognised volunteers in conflict with the police and the British Army as the Irish Republican Army. Violence broke out on 21 July 1920, the first full day back at work after the Twelfth holiday, when 'disloyal' workers – Catholics and socialists – were pelted with rivets and driven out of the shipyards. In the days following, Catholics were also expelled from the Sirocco Works, Mackie's, McLaughlin and Harvey's, Musgrave's and Combe Barbour's, and fierce rioting erupted in many districts, including, as this photograph shows, the city centre.

BELFAST TELEGRAPH

The funeral of the MacMahon family. In the early hours of 24 March 1922 uniformed men, thought to have been RIC, broke into the home of Owen MacMahon, a Catholic publican who lived in Austin Road. Five members of the family were shot dead; only the youngest child, who crept under a table, survived. Altogether sixty-one people in Belfast died in the violence of March 1922. On 31 March a bomb was thrown into the kitchen of a home in Brown Street: Francis Donnelly and his two daughters were severely wounded and his two boys – aged twelve and two years ten months – died from their injuries.

BELFAST TELEGRAPH

OPPOSITE TOP:

Men of the Ulster Special Constabulary setting up a traffic control on the Malone Road, 8 May 1922. In June 1920 the Ulster Unionist Council had agreed to revive the UVF and unauthorised special constables had already been taking action against the IRA in east Belfast and in Fermanagh. The Special Constabulary, set up in October, was divided into three categories: A Specials, numbering 2,000, were to be full-time, uniformed and paid like the Royal Irish Constabulary; B Specials, numbering 19,500, would be part-time, uniformed and unpaid, serving only in their own areas, and armed with weapons kept in police barracks; and an unspecified number of C Specials, an unpaid reserve force identified by caps and armlets.

BELFAST TELEGRAPH

BELOW:

Over fifty Sinn Féin and IRA suspects arrived in Belfast from County Fermanagh on 30 May 1922 under armed guard. Here one of the lorries with prisoners and Special constables leaves the Great Northern Railway station in Great Victoria Street for Belfast Prison on the Crumlin Road. Under the Civil Authorities (Special Powers) Act, internment had been imposed a few days earlier following the murder of W.J. Twaddell, Unionist MP for Woodvale. All two hundred men arrested in the first sweep were Catholics and most were later transferred to an old ship moored in Larne Lough.

BELFAST TELEGRAPH

RIGHT:
Northern Ireland was created by the Government of Ireland Act of 1920 and the first general election was held on Empire Day, 24 May 1921. Forty Unionists, six Nationalists and six Sinn Féin were elected. This photograph shows the first sitting of the parliament in Belfast City Hall on 7 June. Only the Unionists were present since both the nationalist and republican opposition refused to take their seats. George V came to Belfast on 22 June for the official opening ceremony, also in the City Hall.

BELFAST TELEGRAPH

BELOW:
The laying of the foundation stone of Parliament Buildings at Stormont by the Duke of Abercorn, governor of Northern Ireland, in 1928.

PARLIAMENT BUILDINGS,
STORMONT

LEFT:
The construction of Parliament Buildings at Stormont. The finance minister, Hugh Pollock, described it as 'the outward and visible proof of the permanence of our institutions; that for all time we are bound indissolubly to the British crown'. The magnificence of the setting on rising ground was enhanced by grand drives. Designed by Sir Arnold Thornley, Parliament Buildings was erected on a plinth of unpolished Mourne granite and faced in Portland stone. Here we see the west elevation under construction. Before the building was opened by the Prince of Wales in November 1932 the parliament met in the City Hall and in the Presbyterian Assembly College.

CONSARC DESIGN GROUP/
STORMONT LIBRARY

ABOVE:

A Jewish wedding reception for Benny
Spiro and Bessie Berwitz in the Ulster
Hall in 1922. In 1914 Benny Spiro's
address in Hamburg had been used by
Major Fred Crawford as his base for
purchasing 216 tons of arms from
Bruno Spiro for the UVF, landed at
Larne, Bangor and Donaghadee in
April of that year. Bruno Spiro later
died in one of Hitler's death camps.
Jack Lantin had been driven out of
Lithuania during a Tsarist pogrom and
arrived in Belfast to become a partner
with David Spiro in the linen industry.
In 1910 he set up on his own as a
merchant converter, distributing linen
to retailers and placing orders with
manufacturers. Philip Lantin took over
the business and retired in 1992.

PHILIP LANTIN

The workroom in Thorndale House, the Salvation Army's refuge which took in 'fallen'
women who had become pregnant outside wedlock. Here arrangements were made to have
the children adopted and women were trained to become domestic servants. In other
similar institutions in the city unmarried mothers were generally put to work in laundries.

SALVATION ARMY, IRELAND DIVISION

Skipper Street, linking Waring Street to High Street. One of Belfast's oldest streets, it is shown on a
map of 1685 as a row of single-storey cottages on the west side. It was known as Skipars Lean in 1715,
as Skippers Lane in 1767 and as Skipper Street by 1819. Sea captains lodged in the street and in the
nineteenth century two emigration agents and several tea merchants had their premises here. It was
badly damaged during the 1941 German air raids. This photograph was taken from the Waring Street
end in 1927, and the building on the left is the former head office of the Ulster Bank.

ULSTER BANK

RIGHT:
'Hello, hello, this is 2BE, the Belfast station of the British Broadcasting Company, calling.' With these words Tyrone Guthrie made the opening announcement of the BBC in Northern Ireland on 15 September 1924. After a few minutes a technical fault interrupted transmission; when this was remedied music lasting an hour and a half followed and the broadcast ended with a news bulletin and a short speech by the director, Major Walter Scott. This photograph shows the BBC control room above the power station on the Albertbridge Road in 1924.

BBC NI

Tyrone Guthrie, later a theatrical director of international importance, launched his career as a BBC producer in Belfast. Here he is, wearing a white shirt and a bow tie, making an outside broadcast in Linenhall Street in 1928.

NMGNI UM

OPPOSITE BOTTOM:

Gas exhibition in the Ulster Hall in 1924. Gas lighting was introduced in Belfast in 1823, the light being described by the *Belfast News-Letter* as 'resembling the clear effulgence of a cloudless atmosphere illumined by the moon'. Belfast had the cheapest gas in the United Kingdom (with sufficient profits to pay for the building of the City Hall) and its gasworks had in the 1920s the largest spiral-guided gasometer in the world.

LINEN HALL LIBRARY

Brass founding in Combe Barbour's Falls foundry in North Howard Street in 1928. James Combe set up here as a founder and engineer in 1845 and went into partnership fifteen years later with his brother-in-law, James Barbour, a member of the Lisburn linen-thread manufacturing family. Combe invented the grooved pulley for rope driving, widely used across the world before the end of the nineteenth century. The firm vied with Mackie's as a maker of textile machinery and specialised in the manufacture of machines for the preparation and spinning of flax, jute, sisal, hemp rope and cord yarns, and of twisting and laying machinery for twines used by American reapers, binders and combine harvesters. The firm's other products included stretched leather belting, spindles, machine brushes, files and flyers. Though situated in a Catholic district, Combe Barbour's employed very few Catholics after the sectarian expulsions of the summer of 1920.

LEFT:
An early four-colour web-fed letterpress at the Loopbridge works of McCaw, Stevenson and Orr. This machine, similar to a wallpaper printing machine, was used for printing 'glacier' window transparencies, mainly for see-through advertisements and also for decorating windows to give them a stained-glass look.

MSO

BELOW:
Marshall's Tailors. Tailoring required a long apprenticeship but gave work which was considered clean and respectable.

BBC NI

Orange procession, Shaftesbury Square, 1923. The largest procession in Ulster passed through this square every Twelfth of July, and still does: the lodges from different districts converge in the city centre and then march south along the Lisburn Road to the chosen 'field', which usually was in Finaghy. The year 1923 was the first for some time when processions took place in completely peaceful circumstances.

LINEN HALL LIBRARY

May's Market, named after Sir Edward May, who in 1795 had arranged an illegal marriage between his illegitimate daughter and the deeply indebted George Augustus Chichester, then Lord Belfast and later the bankrupt 2nd Marquess of Donegall. This reclaimed slobland was laid out for the sale of farm produce and fodder in the 1850s. The area was completely transformed in the late 1990s to become Lanyon Place, Laganside Corporation's flagship development, including the Waterfront Hall (opened 1997), the five-star Hilton Hotel, the British Telecom Riverside Tower (completed 1998), and as the millennium draws to a close work is well advanced on a £21 million speculative office development by the Oxford Street/East Bridge Street junction. Thanksgiving Square is planned adjacent to the Queen's Bridge: it is a project to bring people together from all communities and backgrounds to reflect and celebrate, and will comprise of a sculptured beacon and landscaped gardens.

BELFAST TELEGRAPH

The ragging of Winston Churchill in front of Queen's University in 1926. Churchill was then in the political doldrums, but he had been forgiven by Ulster Protestants as the minister who had introduced the third Home Rule Bill, because of his later, unswerving support for the Northern Ireland government.

PRONI

Queen's University about 1920. The Tudor revival building had been erected in 1849 to a design by Sir Charles Lanyon. Queen's College had become a university in 1908 and, thanks to an agreement to open a department of scholastic philosophy, Catholic bishops had lifted their ban on Catholics entering the university. Queen's was the only notable interdenominational educational establishment in the city: by 1915, 25 per cent of students were Catholics and, also, in 1911 over a quarter of the 585 students were women.

NMGNI UM

St Mary's College, Falls Road. This teacher-training college for women had been founded on the initiative of Patrick Dorrian, bishop of Down and Connor. At first it was entirely funded by the Catholic Church but in 1911 Westminster had undertaken to pay £1,000 a year, which allowed the Church to recoup its investment. After partition in 1921, out of seven teacher-training institutions in Ireland, St Mary's was the only one which was north of the border. The capitation grant allocated by the ministry of education was the same as that given to female students at Stranmillis College.

ST MARY'S COLLEGE

The main building of Stranmillis College, erected between 1926 and 1929. The hope of the minister of education, Lord Londonderry, that the college would train Protestant and Catholic students together was swiftly dashed by representatives of both denominations. St Mary's, the women's Catholic teacher-training college on the Falls Road, got government support and Catholic male students received grants to attend the Catholic college at Strawberry Hill in Middlesex. The grounds of Stranmillis College remain a notable haven for wildlife in the city and is home to red squirrels, badgers, foxes and jays.

STRANMILLIS UNIVERSITY COLLEGE LIBRARY

58

RIGHT:
Belfast had the first municipal aerodrome in the United Kingdom, opened in upper Malone in 1924. Here Elsie Irvine, who claimed to be the first fare-paying passenger to cross the Irish Sea, is boarding a DH 50 in that year. The pilot was Captain R.H. MacIntosh, known as 'All-weather Mac'.

ERNIE CROMIE, ULSTER
AVIATION SOCIETY

BELOW:
Eason and Son made early use of cross-channel flights to bring over early newspaper editions from London.

EASON & SON NI

BELOW:
A young woman sweeps up outside a café for taxi drivers in Ocean Square, a busy dockland area off Corporation Street. In the late seventeenth century this was the 'Plantation' where William Waring had placed a line of trees; Captain John McCracken's rope walk, established in 1758, passed through here; and in the early twentieth century buildings here, included the Ocean Marine Insurance Company, the National Sailors' and Firemen's Union, and the North Star Hotel. Final traces of Ocean Square and the adjacent Gamble Street were obliterated during 1992 when Dargan Bridge was being constructed.

PRONI

How to navigate the busy intersection at Shaftesbury Square, south of the city centre. This area had been marshland until the middle of the nineteenth century and the main route from Lisburn to the centre of Belfast was through Sandy Row.

Motor cars assemble for a rally in Linenhall Street – a bull-nosed Morris, an Alvis, a Rhode and a Standard amongst others. By 1920 there were thirty-eight motor car agents and hirers in the city. Chambers Brothers made motor cars in Belfast from 1903 but these beautiful and expensive hand-crafted vehicles could not compete with larger producers and the firm ceased manufacture in 1928.

Royal Avenue in 1928. Belfast Corporation had laid down stringent regulations for façades when the street replaced Hercules Lane in the 1880s and 1890s which ensured a degree of symmetry. The first building on the left is the Reform Club, built as a headquarters for the Liberal Party, but since most members were opposed to home rule, Sir Edward Carson was able to make his main speech on Ulster Day, 28 September 1912, from a first-floor window. Next to it is the Grand Central Hotel, demolished in 1983. In the foreground is Castle Place, known to all then as Castle Junction because it was the starting point for most tram journeys.

BELFAST TELEGRAPH

1930s

The last journey of the Bangor Boat on 15 August 1939.
Members of the Grosvenor Hall Methodist congregation
travelled down on this occasion to bid farewell to the Reverend
Ernie Ker who was beginning his journey to the mission fields
on the cross-channel ferry. The Bangor Boat was assigned to
other duties on the outbreak of war less than three weeks later.
Left to right: Mrs Tomlinson; Mrs Dawson;
Mrs Ferguson; Mrs Hutchinson; Mrs Magill; and Mrs Tinman

Harry Ferguson (left) makes a gentleman's agreement with Henry Ford in October 1938. Ferguson, who had been trained at the Municipal Technical Institute, invented the modern tractor. This agreement gave Ford the right to manufacture Ferguson Brown tractors and accessories to Ferguson's specifications and sell them across the world. After the war Ferguson felt that Henry Ford II had reneged on the 'handshake agreement' and took him to court; he won and was paid over £9 million in compensation.

BBC NI

Bellevue in 1934. When Belfast Corporation bought over the Cavehill and Whitewell Tramway in 1911 the assets included thirty-eight acres of woodland which were developed as a recreation ground. It was hoped that the promenade, opened in 1912, with tea rooms and bandstands, would make a profit but the losses were considerable. Zoological Gardens were opened here in 1934, the same year in which Lord Shaftesbury gave Belfast Castle and its grounds to the city. The overall result was that Belfast had a splendid playground in a magnificent setting.

NMGNI UFTM

O N 23 OCTOBER 1929 SECURITY PRICES on the Wall Street stock market crumbled in a wave of frenzied selling and in less than a month the securities lost $26 billion – more than 40 per cent – of their face value. This collapse of business confidence after the great speculative orgy of 1928–9 was followed by an unrelieved world depression lasting ten years. Perhaps no city in the United Kingdom was hit harder than Belfast by this severe contraction in trade. The city was particularly vulnerable because it depended on a limited range of export industries. There was a world surplus of the goods Belfast produced, new competitors and alternative products had emerged and most governments took refuge behind prohibitively high tariff walls and in competitive devaluation which, for example, all but killed Cantrell and Cochrane's and Ross's overseas sales of aerated waters.

A quarter, and sometimes more, of Belfast's insured workers were unemployed in the 1930s and inadequate relief measures provoked the outdoor relief riots of 1932. Deprivation seemed to heighten intercommunal tensions, resulting in sectarian violence in 1935. The city's population continued to grow, from 386,947 in 1911 to 438,086 in 1937; since council house-building virtually came to a halt, citizens were increasingly crammed into overcrowded and ageing dwellings, helping to raise the numbers of those who fell victim to tuberculosis. The opening of the Parliament Buildings at Stormont, too grandiose for a devolved region with a population of only one and a half million, seemed to underline the stark contrast between the haves and the have-nots. The approach of another general European war actually offered the prospect of employment that rearmament would bring.

BELOW:
The official opening of Belfast Harbour Airport alongside the Musgrave Yard at Sydenham by Annie Chamberlain, the wife of Prime Minister Neville Chamberlain, on 16 March 1938. The occasion was marked by a joint air display by Fairey Battle aircraft of number 52 Squadron, Royal Air Force, with Hawker Hind aircraft of number 502 (Ulster) Squadron and the Auxiliary Air Force. The hangar on the left was made by Harland and Wolff and the temporary airport terminal building in the background was never replaced by the proposed permanent structure.
BELFAST TELEGRAPH/ERNIE CROMIE, ULSTER AVIATION SOCIETY

Stones prised from Baker Street ready for use against the police during the outdoor relief riots of 1932, with the twin spires of St Peter's Pro-Cathedral behind. People out of work soon used up their entitlement to the dole and were forced to turn to the workhouse. The outdoor relief provided by the Belfast Board of Guardians was the lowest of that provided in any city of the United Kingdom: payment was in the form of 'chits' for nominated grocery shops; the names of recipients were posted on gable walls; and in order to qualify for help, heavy work – usually resurfacing the streets – had to be undertaken. In October 1932 demonstrations by the unemployed were banned by the government and Catholics and Protestants temporarily sank their differences to combat the RUC. Two men were killed by police gunfire.

LEFT:
Boys being fed by Belfast Central Mission. By 1932 the official unemployment rate had risen to 28 per cent and in September there were 48,000 registered unemployed in Belfast, almost half of whom were not receiving benefit, and of that number 14,500 were not receiving transitional benefit and had therefore to seek outdoor relief. Not a single ship was launched at Queen's Island for two and a half years; the number of employees at Harland and Wolff was reduced from 10,428 in 1930 to 1,554 in 1932; and Workman Clark was forced to close down in 1935.

BELFAST CENTRAL MISSION

BELOW:
Hungry men, women and children queue for food outside Ker Hall, run by Belfast Central Mission, in Glengall Street, during the 1932 outdoor relief crisis.

BELFAST CENTRAL MISSION

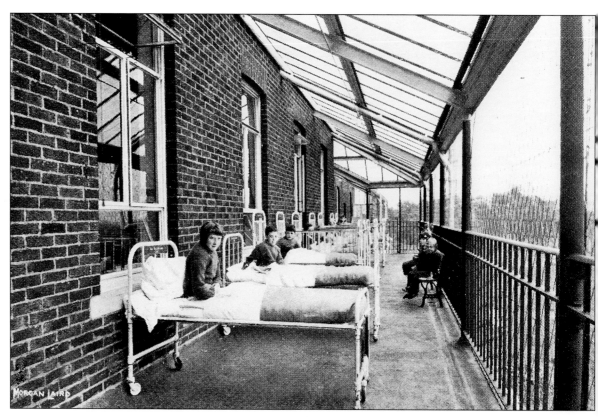

OPPOSITE TOP:
Sick children recuperating on the veranda of the Royal Victoria Hospital. The
Belfast Hospital for Sick Children was opened on the Falls Road in 1932. Lack
of hygiene, poverty and inadequate medical care largely explain why in Belfast
51 per cent of all deaths under fifteen years of age were caused by infectious
diseases – 25 per cent higher than in English boroughs. Whooping cough,
influenza and measles killed around three times as many in Belfast in the late
1930s than in similar cities across the Irish Sea. Pneumonia was the deadliest
disease in Belfast but the main killer of young adults was tuberculosis,
responsible for 49 per cent of all deaths in the age group 15 to 25 and for 38
per cent of those between 25 and 35. The mortality rate from tuberculosis was
20 per cent higher in Northern Ireland than in the rest of the United Kingdom.

ROYAL BELFAST HOSPITAL FOR SICK CHILDREN

BELOW:
Sewer pipes being laid in Sussex Street. The Silent Valley reservoir was
completed in 1933, a huge undertaking for the Belfast Water Commissioners
which took ten years and increased the supply each day to 21 million gallons.
Ultimately this was of great benefit to citizens but improvement in public health
was slow. When compared with six British cities, Belfast had the lowest infant
mortality rate in 1901 but in 1938 it had the highest rate, 96 per 1,000 live
births compared with, for example, 59 in Sheffield.

NMGNI UM

ABOVE:
The arrival of the Prince of Wales in a cavalcade of cars down Royal Avenue and Donegall Place in November 1932. The prince had come for the formal opening of the Northern Ireland parliament's permanent home at Stormont in east Belfast (RIGHT). According to St John Ervine, playwright and biographer of Prime Minister Lord Craigavon, the prince performed the ceremony with 'an unsmiling face and glum and sulky looks'. Afterwards, however, he enjoyed his attempt to play a Lambeg drum. Nationalists refused to attend and they were even less inclined to end their fitful abstention when in the following year the prime minister said: 'In the South they boasted of a Catholic state. They still boast of Southern Ireland being a Catholic State. All I boast is that we are a Protestant Parliament and a Protestant State.'

BELFAST TELEGRAPH

Empty slips at Harland and Wolff. Orders generated in earlier confident years delayed the impact of the slump on Queen's Island, which was busier than at any time since the post-war boom. Then, shipping rates sagged catastrophically, the Union-Castle Line cancelled its repair contracts with Harland and Wolff, and the company's accounts were so appalling for 1931 that they were not published until September 1932. Not a single ship was launched at Queen's Island between 10 December 1931 and 1 May 1934.

NMGNI UFTM

RIGHT:
Joseph Devlin (1871–1934), leader of the Nationalist Party. Entering Westminster for the first time for North Kilkenny in 1902, he wrested West Belfast from the Unionists by a narrow margin in 1906 and became the principal spokesman for northern nationalists. Following the triumph of Sinn Féin in 1918, he became the leader of the six remaining Nationalist MPs. Opposed to partition as he was, he felt that Nationalists should represent their constituents in the Northern Ireland parliament and took his seat in 1925. Intense frustration and Unionist triumphalism caused him to withdraw periodically thereafter.

BELFAST CENTRAL LIBRARY

BELOW:
Decorations to celebrate the Eucharistic Congress in a side street off the Falls Road, June 1932, the thirty-first in a series of international congresses organised by the Catholic Church for the promotion of devotion to the Blessed Sacrament. The pope sent over Lorenzo Lauri as his cardinal legate and the high point was the celebration of mass in Dublin's Phoenix Park. Thousands of northern Catholics travelled to Dublin and Catholic towns and districts were decorated for the event. The Northern Ireland cabinet concluded that the congress had created 'excitement amounting almost to frenzy' and special trains returning with pilgrims were attacked at stations and in particular at the Great Northern Railway terminus in Great Victoria Street.

DOWN AND CONNOR DIOCESAN ARCHIVES

The Hawthornden gate lodge of Campbell College after an IRA attack. In 1935 the Belfast IRA carefully planned a raid on the Officers' Training Corps armoury of this exclusive boys' secondary school in east Belfast but it was clear that the RUC had been tipped off. After a sustained gun battle on 27 December, the attackers were driven off. Four men were arrested and Edward MacCartney, the only man tried and convicted, received ten years. During an IRA court martial to investigate the reasons for the failure of the raid in the Craobh Ruadh Club in Crown Entry on 25 April 1936 the police swooped and arrested twelve leading members. Charged in Belfast with treason-felony, they received a total of forty-eight years' penal servitude.

CAMPBELL COLLEGE

Houses in the York Street area burned during the 1935 riots. Feelings ran high in Belfast when Protestants triumphantly celebrated George V's jubilee in June 1935. The Ministry of Home Affairs banned all parades but this was lifted after protests. Rioting began towards the close of the Twelfth parade in Lancaster Street and the violence continued in the York Street area until the end of August, by which time eight Protestants and five Catholics had been killed. The great majority of the wounded were Catholic; over 2,000 Catholics and a handful of Protestants were driven from their homes; and 95 per cent of the £21,669 compensation for destruction to property was paid out to Catholics.

Willowfield Unionist Club and the picture house, popularly known as the 'Winkie', on the Woodstock Road. In 1935 Belfast had 31 cinemas, with seating for a total of 28,000 people, that is 1 seat for every 15 of the population. The 'Winkie' opened in 1915 and, like most cinemas, had a separate entrance for the cheaper front stall seats.

PRONI

The Ritz Cinema, Fisherwick Place, when it was opened by Gracie Fields in November 1936. The largest cinema in Northern Ireland, it had seating for 2,200 people, a Compton organ which rose out of the pit and a luxurious café.

NMGNI UM

Custom House Square Gardens. Originally at the back, and now next to the entrance of, the Custom House, this area was reclaimed from the Lagan estuary in 1757 and part of it was used as salt pans, managed by Daniel Mussenden. Ten years later ships were being built, and lime and salt were being made here, presumably with the aid of imported coal. From the banks of a pond where the Custom House now stands, cod and whiting 'were caught in abundance by the line'. A map of 1791 shows that the Ballast Office (later pulled down to make way for the Custom House) had been put up on dry land between Limekiln Dock and Chichester Quay. Not until the docks had been filled in (becoming Queen's Square and Albert Square) was it possible to build the Custom House and the remaining land could be laid out as a square. This was still a busy dockland area in the 1930s with warehouses, bonded stores, and importers' and exporters' offices. The White Star Line, Harland and Wolff's main customer, was unable to weather the tempests dislocating world trade and Cunard henceforth dominated the British transatlantic passenger business.

PRONI

ABOVE:
By Molly Ward's, the first lock from the sea on the Lagan Canal. Belfast was still a very compact city and here at Stranmillis these boys could feel that they were in the country. In *As I Roved Out*, Cathal O'Byrne wrote: 'The green willow shadows and the green water met and blended where the sun-dazzle made lovelier all the waving green waterway. All was still, save where a rush of seething waters passed over the weir and wove in their passing a breadth of silver tissue fine as spider's spinning. In all this northern land there is no lovelier place for a summer ramble than round by the Lagan water up at Molly Ward's.'

PRONI

The Cavehill Waterworks on the Antrim Road. This was one of a series of reservoirs built close to Belfast by the Water Commissioners. It proved acutely difficult to keep such a rapidly growing city supplied and it was not until water began to arrive from the Mourne Mountains in 1901 that the problem was solved. Permission to fish for trout here was given only to ratepayers. It seems likely that the Cavehill Waterworks were mistaken for the docks by German bombers in 1941 and this partly explains the high death toll in this area in the Easter Tuesday raid.

PRONI

LEFT AND ABOVE:
Skiing and sleighing on the Ballysillan Road. Ireland's temperate climate provided few enough opportunities for these winter sports but there were generally several days each year during which snow lay deep enough to get out sledges, often quickly constructed from orange boxes. Snow lay longest on the northern- and eastern-facing slopes of the edge of the basalt escarpment overlooking north Belfast and Glengormley, which some would argue possess their own microclimate.

PRONI

Public baths at Peter's Hill, at the foot of the Shankill Road. These were the first to be provided in Belfast, built in 1879 by the corporation. Three more were constructed: Ormeau Avenue Baths in 1888; Templemore Avenue Baths in 1893; and the Falls Road Baths in 1896. There were two swimming pools in each but in Templemore and Falls the second-class ponds were converted into gymnasia in the winter. Between the wars a high but unmeasured number of dwellings in Belfast possessed outside toilets only and had no baths. As a result public baths provided an essential facility for many citizens in the 1930s.

PRONI

Football in Ormeau Park in 1937. Except on the outskirts, Belfast was poorly provided with public parks with the result that Ormeau, Dunville, Falls, Victoria and Woodvale parks were heavily used. After the death, in 1844, of the profligate 2nd Marquess of Donegall, who had resided at Ormeau, his property was put into the hands of the receiver and the freehold of Belfast was disposed of. Ormeau was abandoned, the house was demolished, and the corporation bought the estate to create a park in 1870.

PRONI

LEFT:
A match between North (North of Ireland Cricket Club) and Cliftonville in 1937. Cricket was brought to Belfast by troops stationed in the city and by factory owners who had been educated in English public schools. North won ten out of twenty-eight competitions before 1914 but between the wars faced stiff competion from North Down and later from Woodvale, Waringstown and Lisburn.

PRONI

A game at the Oval, 1937. This was the home ground of the east Belfast team, Glentoran. The thirties were good years for the 'Glens', who won the Irish Cup in 1932, 1933 and 1935 – a prize they would not seize again until 1951. Their most dazzling player in this decade was Johnny Geary, who scored forty-eight goals in his first season.

PRONI

RIGHT:
Rinty Monaghan training in Hardinge Street. Born John Joseph Monaghan in 1920, he began his boxing career in Ma Copley's boxing booth and became Belfast's greatest sporting hero when on 23 March 1948 he won the world flyweight championship by knocking out Jackie Patterson in the King's Hall. Two years later he retired undefeated. He also held the British, European and Commonwealth championships and out of fifty-four professional fights he lost only eight, drew three and won forty-three. He died in his native city in 1984.

PRONI

BELOW:
The O'Donovan Rossa GAA hurling team in 1935. The club first won the County Antrim senior championships in hurling in 1918 and in 1919 and were winners on twelve further occasions. It also won the County Antrim senior championships in gaelic football fourteen times. The club's grounds are at Shaw's Road and its social centre is at 506 Falls Road – now called Rossa House, its first owner was Colonel Robert Baden-Powell, the hero of the siege of Mafeking and founder of the Boy Scout movement.

O'DONOVAN ROSSA GAC

Ice skating at the King's Hall, Balmoral Show Grounds. The King's Hall was named by the command of George V and was opened by the Duke of Gloucester on 29 May 1934. It cost £60,000 to build and could seat 12,500 people. The hall was an ideal venue for boxing matches, concerts and large exhibitions and was for long the only place in Northern Ireland with a skating rink.

PRONI

Eason and Son, Lower Donegall Street, 1936

EASON & SON NI

Campbell College in east Belfast was one of the few institutions which took seriously the threat of aerial bombardment, and here pupils are taking part in a practice evacuation to the school's air-raid shelter. In 1940 the college was commissioned by the government as number 24 General Hospital and boarding pupils were sent to the Northern Counties Hotel in Portrush. The school, possibly mistaken for Stormont, was hit during the raid of 4–5 May 1941 and nineteen patients and medical staff were killed when Nissen huts at the rear of the college were blown apart.

CAMPBELL COLLEGE

Bristol Bombay L5808 being hauled out for display on 4 March 1939, the first aircraft to be built at the Short and Harland factory. This combined bomber and transport aeroplane had been designed by the Bristol Company but was made in Belfast because at that time the firm lacked the capacity to build them. Fifty of these RAF bombers were eventually manufactured, all of them in Belfast.

ERNIE CROMIE, ULSTER AVIATION SOCIETY

1940s

'ALL SORTS OF ROT GOING ON HERE,' Lady Londonderry wrote to her husband soon after the outbreak of war in 1939. 'Air raid warnings and blackouts! As if anyone cared or wished to bomb Belfast.' Most people in the city and some government ministers agreed with this view. Indeed, international conflict promised the revival of industries which had languished for almost two decades and contracts for ships, vessel refitting, ropes and cordage, bomber aircraft, uniforms and canvas, and other war material offered new hope to those who had been out of work for so long.

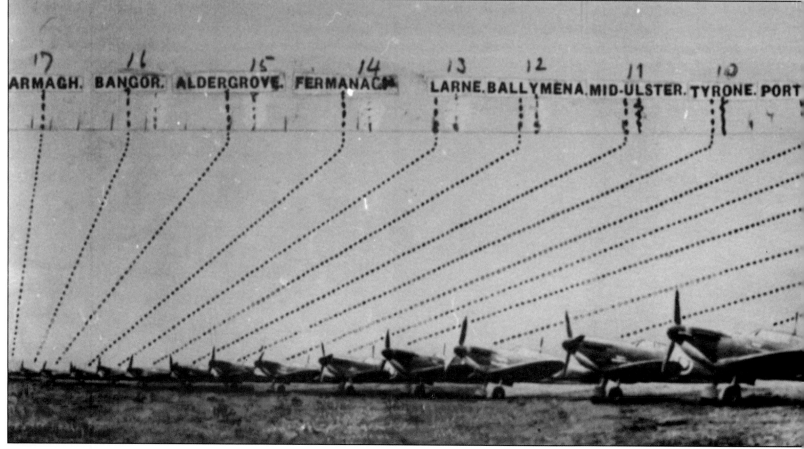

17 ARMAGH. 16 BANGOR. 15 ALDERGROVE. 14 FERMANAGH. 13 LARNE. 12 BALLYMENA. 11 MID-ULSTER. 10 TYRONE. PORT

OPPOSITE:
Children in Memel Street, Bridge
End, collect scrap metal and waste
paper for the war effort in 1940.
They were responding to an appeal
issued by the Ministry of Commerce:
'Waste Wanted for War Weapons. Put
out PAPER because it is wanted for
food containers, cases for shells and
other vital needs. Put out METAL
because it means more guns. Tanks,
ships and munitions of all kinds need
metal. So collect every scrap of it.
Remember always to put out the
PAPER and the METAL separately
beside your dustbin. They *will* be
collected and they *will* be used.
They are wanted urgently.'

BELFAST TELEGRAPH

On the afternoon of 30 November 1940 a single, unobserved German plane flew high over Belfast and later examination of the high-definition photographs in Germany revealed that the city was defended by only seven anti-aircraft batteries. By this stage France had fallen, the United Kingdom was fighting alone and, as the Luftwaffe pounded British cities every night, it was becoming too late for the corporation and the Stormont government to make up for their previous disregard of the people's safety. The German air raids of April and May 1941 killed well over a thousand citizens and left much of the inner city in a state of devastation.

Belfast's recovery began when Hitler attacked Russia in June 1941: the first Americans arrived in the city on 26 January 1942, and unemployment disappeared as Belfast responded to the urgent demands of the Allied war machine. The post-war boom was carefully controlled and for the remainder of the decade Belfast's traditional export industries showed remarkable vigour as they strove to meet the shortages of a European mainland ravaged by total war. The shared experience of blitz and privation had only papered over intercommunal divisions, however, and elections fought in 1949 were the most bitter and violent seen in the city since 1921.

The seventeen Spitfires bought with funds raised through the *Belfast Telegraph*. Major William Baird, the newspaper's managing director, launched the fund on 12 August 1940 as the Battle of Britain began in earnest, with the aim of raising £5,000 – the cost of one plane – in shillings, 'to enable the humblest in the country to share in a project . . . at this time of national peril'. Contributions exceeded all expectations: £2,559 on the first day; £51,000 by the end of the first year; and £88,633 16s. 5d. by 23 May 1945.

BELFAST TELEGRAPH

Before the war it was planned to evacuate 70,000 children from Belfast but it was not until July 1940 that a scheme was adopted to take 17,000 out of the city. Only 7,000 children turned up, followed by 1,800 six weeks later, and more than half those evacuated had returned by the spring of 1941. However, after the air raids of April and May 1941 the exodus from Belfast was on a huge scale and the minister of public security, John MacDermott, observed that more were leaving 'in proportion to population than any other city in the United Kingdom'. By 3 May 1941 it was estimated that 100,000 people – around one-quarter of the population of Belfast – had fled to the Northern Ireland countryside.

BELFAST TELEGRAPH

LEFT:
Women in Belfast had long been employed in linen mills and weaving factories but during the war large numbers were engaged in engineering shops, in what was generally considered 'men's work'. However, equal work did not mean equal pay, though many supervisors considered women to be faster and more accurate, particularly in precision work.

PRONI

BELOW:
After the Easter Tuesday raid of 15–16 April 1941 the government ordered that an attempt be made to camouflage the Parliament Buildings at Stormont. This photograph shows the white Portland stone coated with pitch. The approach roads were strewn with cinders. Citizens would have been appalled if they had known how much time was spent at cabinet meetings discussing the protection of Stormont and the statue of Edward Carson (visible at the end of the road) at a time when 40,000 people had to be put up in rest centres and 70,000 had to be given meals every day in emergency feeding centres.

NMGNI UFTM

ABOVE:
Arnott's department store at the corner of High Street and Bridge Street in flames after the air raid of 4–5 May 1941. War correspondent Ernst von Kuhren, flying with one Luftwaffe squadron, broadcast his impressions: 'When we approached the target at half-past two we stared silently into a sea of flames such as none of us had seen before . . . In Belfast there was not a large number of conflagrations, but just one enormous conflagration which spread over the entire harbour and industrial area.' In fact, a great many commercial properties in the city centre and houses in east Belfast were also destroyed.

NMGNI UM

RIGHT:
The London, Midland and Scottish railway station after the 4–5 May raid. Struck by bombs and incendiaries, fire swept through the station, destroying coaches, engines, offices, sheds and stores. The nearby Midland Hotel was also gutted.

BELFAST TELEGRAPH

BELOW:
The York Street mill had been the largest linen-spinning mill in the world. It was destroyed during the Easter Tuesday raid on 15–16 April 1941. 'It was as if a great hand had sliced down at an angle, cutting it in two,' Jim McConville remembered. The collapsing six storeys obliterated forty-two houses, and damaged twenty-one, in Sussex Street and Vere Street. The mill was struck again on 4–5 May, and in what may have been the biggest single fire during that raid, the entire works were destroyed.

BELFAST TELEGRAPH

RIGHT:
Repairs under way on the roof of the City Hall, 3 June 1941. During the air raid of 4–5 May the banqueting hall was badly damaged and cracks can still be seen in the building to this day. Other buildings destroyed in the city centre included an eighteenth-century church in Rosemary Street, the roof and much of the interior of the Water Commissioners' Office, Arnott's, Gallaher's and Dunville's. There was widespread looting afterwards and the entire stock and fixtures screwed to the counter were removed from a public house in Callender Street.

NMGNI UM

Bombed buildings in Lower Donegall Street still smouldering after the 4–5 May raid. St Anne's Church of Ireland Cathedral was fortunate to survive attack.

The corner of Bridge Street and High Street being cleared after the raid of 4–5 May 1941. This became known as Blitz Square. In the foreground a static water tank is under construction.

RIGHT:
Templemore Avenue after the air raid of 4–5 May 1941. This street in east Belfast and the area around it suffered severely; after the war Rupert Stanley College was built on a site created by the destruction of rows of terraced housing at the Newtownards Road end of the avenue. This photograph shows the damage inflicted on the Ulster Hospital in Templemore Avenue. On duty that night, surgeon M.I. McClure realised that the bombs were falling in such rapid succession that the hospital could not escape: 'The building at this stage was beginning to shake and tremble with each explosion [and when the hospital was struck] we tried to use our internal hoses but the water mains must have been struck and no water came through . . . one fairly large bomb fell on and through the roof, immediately the area burst into flames.'

PRONI

BELOW:
Hughenden Avenue, Cavehill Road, showing damage inflicted by the Easter Tuesday air raid. This became one of several routes to the slopes of Cave Hill where thousands slept in the open every night in case the Germans returned. The German-controlled Radio Paris informed its listeners in the middle of May 1941: 'Fearing air raids, 20,000 women and children escape every evening from Belfast to the outskirts of the city.' In fact, this was a considerable underestimate.

BELFAST TELEGRAPH

Westbourne Street, Newtownards Road, after the blitz of 4–5 May
1941. The residential district that suffered most in this raid was east
Belfast, extending from Sydenham to Ballymacarrett. In Chater Street
not a single house was left standing and at Witham Street, where
thirty-five houses were destroyed, a delayed-action bomb went off
killing nine people. In Avondale Street a parachute mine fell close to a
public shelter and killed twenty-five people taking refuge there. The
ambulance depot on the Holywood Road received a direct hit and
M.I. McClure, a surgeon at the Ulster Hospital in Templemore
Avenue, recalled: 'The first bomb to fall near us fell at 1.05 a.m. . . .
Within a few minutes they seemed to be falling all the time . . . one
had not the time to remove one's steel helmet to adjust the chin strap
before another fell.'

PRONI

Assessing the damage to Stirling bombers at the Short and Harland factory after the air raid of 4–5 May 1941. About one week's output was lost on this site and work soon resumed here using converted bicycle sheds to accommodate plant and machinery. The devastation of the aircraft shop at Harland and Wolff's Alexandra Works, however, prevented parts being made there until 12 June.

BOMBARDIER AEROSPACE

The Germans came close to complete success on the night of 4–5 May when their bombers targeted Harland and Wolff. The Luftwaffe attacked the yard in formation with groups of five bombers taking part in each assault, beginning with incendiary bombs and followed by parachute mines and high explosives. Three corvettes close to completion were destroyed at the Musgrave Channel; *Fairhead*, a transport ship laden with munitions, was sunk at its moorings in the Victoria Channel by a parachute mine; the company records were lost; the electrical mechanical shop, engine works, stores, sheds and drawing offices were destroyed; and altogether almost two-thirds of Harland and Wolff's premises were devastated.

NMGNI UFTM

American football at Ravenhill. By May 1942 the number of Americans in Northern Ireland had reached 37,000. Some moved on in the autumn of 1942 to North Africa for the invasion of Italy; and more arrived in 1943 – raising the number of American troops in Northern Ireland for a time to 120,000 – to prepare for the Normandy landings the following year. Handsome GIs bearing Hershey bars, gum and nylons were a great hit with the girls but young men were less enthusiastic: Jimmy Penton remembers that in east Belfast Americans were 'warned off' Dee Street and 'never came near it'.

PRONI

The first American troops to arrive in Europe stepped ashore at Belfast's Dufferin Quay on 26 January 1942. The band of the Royal Ulster Rifles played 'The Star-spangled Banner' and the *Belfast Telegraph* reported: 'Many of the Americans had thought that at the beginning in camp they would have to live "rough", and they were pleasantly surprised . . . The inevitable dog mascot has made its appearance, an American soldier somehow managing to bring along a mongrel known as "Jitterbug".'

BELFAST TELEGRAPH

Lorry with petrol bombs for use in Allied air raids. These 'jettisonable tanks' were made at the Nicholson and Bass factory in Alfred Street. Incendiaries of this type created terrible fire storms in cities such as Hamburg, and three assaults on Dresden, lasting no more than seventy minutes in all, caused the death of over 100,000 German civilians.

BASS PACKAGING

A huge water tank at the bottom of High Street in March 1944. There was some anxiety that the stagnant water would endanger public health. In Belfast it was largely a case of shutting the stable door after the horse had bolted: the physical protection given to citizens before the blitz was pitifully inadequate, and elaborate measures taken thereafter were unnecessary because the main theatres of conflict shifted elsewhere after Hitler's invasion of Russia in June 1941 and the entry of the United States into the war in December 1941.

NMGNI UFTM

ABOVE:
Wings for Victory Week, April 1943, at Blitz Square on the corner of High Street and Bridge Street. On the left a Stirling bomber and, right, a Halifax bomber. By now the tide of war had turned: Ulster-born Field Marshal Montgomery had routed Rommel at El Alamein, the Americans had won notable naval victories in the Coral Sea and Midway, the Russians had killed or captured over 300,000 Germans at Stalingrad, and the Allied invasion of Italy was about to begin.
ERNIE CROMIE, ULSTER AVIATION SOCIETY

LEFT:
Queen's University quadrangle. Northern Ireland made a vital contribution towards the food supplies in British cities. Sir Basil Brooke, minister of agriculture until he became prime minister in 1943, set himself the target of increasing the ploughed area of the region to 250,000 acres. He ordered that potatoes, carrots and cabbage be grown in lazy beds on the Stormont estate; he got golf clubs to grow corn on their fairways; and he persuaded Queen's University to cultivate its lawns.

QUEEN'S UNIVERSITY BELFAST

A children's victory party in Medway Street. The *Belfast Telegraph* reported: 'Huge bonfires blazed in many parts of the city and around them bands of young people danced in jubilant mood right into the early hours of the morning.' Dozens of effigies of Hitler were burned on lamp standards. On the Shore Road a bugle band led a procession of youngsters carrying an effigy of the Führer, wearing his swastika and hanging from a gallows. At 10.40 p.m. the City Hall was floodlit for the first time in six years and there was a tremendous cheer as the illumination was switched on

BELFAST TELEGRAPH

VE Day, 8 May 1945, in front of the City Hall. On the evening of 7 May news spread
that the Germans would surrender at midnight. The *Belfast News-Letter* described how
people poured into the city centre to celebrate: 'Along Donegall Place and Royal
Avenue, long lines of revellers joined in snake-like formation, dancing in and out among
rows of tramcars immobilised by the crowds. Songs were in the air everywhere.' At noon
next day the Ulster United Prayer Movement held a victory thanksgiving service in the
grounds of the City Hall and soon afterwards a huge crowd of civilians and servicemen
filled Donegall Square and Donegall Place as Belfast echoed to the celebratory sound of
church bells, ships' sirens and factory hooters. Then a great hush fell as Churchill's
victory broadcast was relayed from the City Hall.

BELFAST TELEGRAPH

Joan Frank, the first woman newsreader in the BBC.

BBC NI

The McCooeys, written by Joseph Tomelty, ran from 1949 to 1955 and was one of the most popular radio serials ever broadcast from Belfast. As soon as its signature tune, 'My Aunt Jane', started up, thousands of people were sitting by their radios, and characters like grocer Bobby Greer and Derek the window cleaner (played by James Young) quickly made the programme compulsive listening.

BBC NI

The end of another day's work at Queen's Island: after throwing in their 'boards', men run to catch their trams. Many workers dreaded a post-war contraction but, thanks in part to Marshall Aid, there was no slump; there were rarely fewer than 20,000 men employed at the yard, which remained the largest shipbuilding unit in the world. As shipping companies strove to replace wartime losses, Harland and Wolff regularly launched over 100,000 tons a year. The Admiralty gave the firm contracts for three aircraft carriers – *Eagle*, *Centaur* and *Bulwark* – and the drive to complete them was increased with the outbreak of the Korean War in 1950.

Trams were already on the way out. By 1947 they were no longer to be seen on the Donegall Road and Cliftonville routes, but the 'Island' trams continued to run until February 1954.

BBC NI

A 'Brother Man' dinner in the Ker Memorial Hall in the Grosvenor Road complex, Christmas 1941. The removal of the Poor Law in 1948 and the introduction of more comprehensive welfare legislation eliminated stark poverty but pockets of severe unemployment and deprivation remained in Belfast. Unskilled workers had lower wages than those in comparable cities in Britain, though the margin was decreasing.

BELFAST CENTRAL MISSION

1950s

I N RETROSPECT, THIS WAS THE MOST PEACEFUL DECADE BELFAST enjoyed in the twentieth century. These years also saw a spectacular improvement in quality of life, despite the people's later tendencies to look back on the fifties as somewhat grey, unadventurous and uneventful. While the city's traditional industries suffered some difficulties, there was no severe slump and at the end of the decade major international firms were starting up business in Greater Belfast. The dramatic welfare reforms brought in by Clement Attlee's Labour government after 1945 were not undone by the Conservatives and Westminster continued largely to underwrite the cost.

Belfast Corporation, put into commission for three and a half years in 1942 due to its refusal to tackle corruption, made strenuous efforts to make up for past neglect. The proportion of Belfast's housing stock destroyed or badly damaged by Luftwaffe bombs – 53.3 per cent – was higher than average compared to blitz damage in other United Kingdom cities. From 1945 to

OPPOSITE:
Boys at the window of Mullan's book shop in Donegall Place. Belfast's premier book shop for many decades, Mullan's was regarded as something of an institution by the city's reading public. The firm went out of business in the 1980s.

IRISH NEWS

RIGHT:
Rock 'n' roll reaches Belfast. The V-2 skiffle group from St Malachy's includes men who were to make their mark on the city: Michael Burns (left), publisher and businessman, Bernard MacLaverty (centre back), writer of short stories, novels and screenplays, and painter Joe McWilliams (right).

JOE McWILLIAMS

RIGHT:
A family just arrived from India in 1953 pose for a formal photograph to send back to relatives on the sub-continent. From left to right: Dwarka Nath Kapur, who became a medical consultant, Phulan Rani Kapur and their three children. Kapur explained later: 'My main reason for coming to Northern Ireland from India was so that I could give my children a fine education. In India, British education was thought to be the best in the world.' In contrast with British cities of similar size, such as Leicester, Belfast attracted very few immigrants from the Indian sub-continent until the 1990s. The Chinese formed the largest Asian community in the city and people came to appreciate the wonderful new cuisine their restaurants offered.

PROFESSOR NARINDER KAPUR

1954, 11,000 dwellings were built in and around Belfast, 6,500 by the Northern Ireland Housing Trust and the corporation's 'Hustle the Houses' committee. By the end of the decade three-quarters of the land surface of the borough of Belfast was built over: for the first time the city was running out of building sites and the radical rethinking that was to lead to the controversial Matthew Stop Line had begun.

Despite unedifying Church disputes over control and religious education, new schools opened to provide young people with free secondary education for the first time. The National Health Service, introduced in Northern Ireland in 1949, had a more profound impact than elsewhere in the United Kingdom because it swept away the niggardly and humiliating Poor Law. By the end of the decade the scourge of tuberculosis had all but been wiped out and prospects for citizens looked better than they had ever been.

RIGHT:
A street party on the Shankill Road celebrating the coronation of Queen Elizabeth II in 1953. This was a particularly calm period in the history of Belfast and such displays of loyalty, while not shared by the Catholic minority, did not cause unrest, unlike the jubilee celebrations of 1935. Despite periodic bouts of unemployment, the Shankill was a thriving community and large numbers came in to shop there from the neighbouring Falls on Saturday afternoons.

BELFAST TELEGRAPH

OPPOSITE BOTTOM:
A trade union demonstration protesting against job losses in the textile industry. For most of the 1940s the only brake on the city's linen industry seemed to be shortage of raw material. A downswing in the industry in 1949 was quickly reversed by the outbreak of the Korean War the following year. Then in 1953 that war came to an end and prices all but collapsed. This was no temporary downturn and one by one great linen houses closed with the loss of around 25,000 jobs between 1951 and 1958.

IRISH PRESS

RIGHT:

A new boat for Kelly's, Belfast's leading coal importers, in November 1952. Sir Samuel Kelly, who had helped to run guns for the UVF in 1914, had installed the most modern equipment and brought over miners from Cumberland and Scotland to exploit coal seams at Coalisland, County Tyrone, in the 1920s in an attempt to replace imported supplies, but severe faulting made the operation uneconomic. *An Economic Survey of Northern Ireland*, a report by K.S. Isles and Norman Cuthbert published in 1957, effectively exposed a coal ring in Belfast; an unreasonable freight charge of 15s.5d. per ton, for example, was added to the Scottish price of 63s. 'The price may also be excessive because of the exercise of monopoly power in fixing the freight rates for the cross-channel shipment,' they concluded and recommended investigation by the Monopolies Commission.

LINEN HALL LIBRARY

BELOW:

The launch of the *Beaverbank* by Harland and Wolff in 1952. Given added stimulus by the Korean War, the shipbuilding industry in Belfast appeared to be flourishing. In 1951, 21,000 men had been kept fully employed; thirteen ships had been built at Queen's Island, including the *Juan Peron*, the world's largest whale factory ship, and the aircraft carrier *Eagle*, the largest vessel in the Royal Navy, had left Belfast Lough on 30 October. However, this warning was given by the *Belfast Telegraph* on 3 January 1952: 'In the future British shipbuilders may be faced with intense competition from Germany and Japan. Allied controls on shipbuilding in Germany were lifted in April, and strenuous efforts are being made to restore the industry in that country to its former prosperity. Japan may eventually be an even more formidable rival than Germany, because she is able to draw upon large reserves of cheap labour.'

LINEN HALL LIBRARY

A Short's VTOL (vertical take-off and landing) aircraft demonstrating its versatility in 1959. Short and Harland, which became Short Brothers in 1947 when the Rochester works closed down, had developed the Sealand flying boat after the Second World War and built more than 130 Canberra bombers during the Korean War. In the 1950s the firm's Seacat and Tigercat anti-aircraft missiles were particularly successful but this 'flying bedstead' – the first of its kind – did not immediately generate orders.

BOMBARDIER AEROSPACE

Unloading timber at the Pollock Basin in 1959. Belfast remained a great port and handled 5 million tons of imports and exports, for example, in 1956, and there were daily cargo and passenger sailings to Heysham, Liverpool and Glasgow. Traditionally, Catholics worked at the deep-sea docks and Protestants at the cross-channel quays but the process which would deprive them of their work had already begun in the 1950s: roll-on/roll-off container services got going at the end of the decade and ten years later container traffic handled by the port of Belfast rose to 1.35 million tons a year.

PRONI

ABOVE:

Inside the *Princess Victoria*. During an acute shortage of milk in Britain in 1949, the *Princess Victoria*, a mail and road vehicle ferry, was taken over by the Ministry of Food to operate twenty-four hours a day carrying 20,000 gallons each trip to Stranraer. The ship's captain, James Ferguson, said: 'This ship alone carries the week's milk ration for one out of every forty people in the country'.

PRONI

RIGHT:

Survivors from the *Princess Victoria*, which sank off the Copeland Islands early in the afternoon of 31 January 1953. That morning the vessel had nosed its way out of Stranraer for Larne into a violent gale, with winds gusting up to 120 miles per hour. As one survivor, Fusilier Walter Baker, said soon afterwards: 'The *Princess Victoria* took a terrific beating from the mountainous seas as soon as she left Loch Ryan. Finally, one very high wave burst open the ramp doors at the stern used for loading vehicles, and the water poured in. The ship took a list and then we realised that we were in a serious position.' The radio officer immediately sent out an SOS but at 1.25 p.m. the ship sank; her master, Captain James Ferguson, went down, one hand held stiffly in salute. A total of 128 people perished in the disaster.

PRONI

LEFT:
Lord Brookeborough, prime minister of Northern Ireland between 1943 and 1963, enjoying a performance. Once the war was over, Brookeborough presided over the most peaceful period in the city's history when intercommunal tensions eased to some degree. He was not, however, prepared to risk alienating the Unionist Party's traditional support by straying from the traditional path. He denounced a proposal made in 1959, endorsed by his attorney-general, Brian Maginess, to allow Catholics to join his party: 'If that is called intolerance, I say at once it is not the fault of the Unionist Party. If it is called inflexible then it shows that our principles are not elastic.'

PRONI

BELOW:
The Queen and the Duke of Edinburgh with Boy Scouts at Balmoral, July 1953. The Boy Scouts, like the Girl Guides, Girls' Brigade and Boys' Brigade, were Protestant organisations, since Catholics had their own parallel youth movements.

PRONI

OPPOSITE:
The Antique Room in the College of Technology's School of Art where students perfected their drawing skills by copying classical statues. Former students included the sculptors Rosamond Praeger, F.E. McWilliam and George MacCann, and the painters Paul Henry, Frank McKelvey, William Conor, John Luke, Colin Middleton, Gerard Dillon, Daniel O'Neill, Maurice Wilks and Rowel Friers. In 1968 a separate College of Art was opened in York Street on a site devastated by the German air raids of 1941.

PRONI

LEFT:
A loom in the textile room in the College of Technology, College Square East. Since 1907 apprentices and engineers had been trained in this building to acquire essential skills in the industry which was still Belfast's largest employer of labour in the early 1950s. This decade, however, saw a dramatic and permanent contraction in the linen industry in the face of competition from synthetic fibres and cheap cotton from overseas.

PRONI

Naval architecture at the College of Technology. First known as the Municipal Technical Institute, this five-storey baroque building in Portland stone, completed in 1907, brought together classes previously housed in premises across the city. Engineers and craftsmen were trained here, who went on to design great ocean liners, marine engines and textile machinery; artists who created designs for damask and embroidered linen and for the city's large printing works; and sculptors, fine carpenters and ironworkers. At first all the staff and virtually all the students were Protestant, with the result that the Catholic Church set up a trades school in Hardinge Street run by the Christian Brothers. By the 1950s there was mounting evidence that Belfast was failing to keep abreast of the latest technological advances, with a few exceptions, notably in aircraft design.

PRONI

The machine room in the Waring Street offices of the Ulster Bank around 1950. The women in the row nearest the camera are (left to right) Kay Dunlop, Vera McDowell and Olive Kinch, and they are using NCR Class 32 accounting machines, first introduced in 1946 and used for many years thereafter before computerisation. As in the civil service and several other professions, women had to resign when they married. In the foreground is a ledger bucket designed by George Millar, used throughout the bank before automation.

ULSTER BANK

LEFT:
Sorting pearls at McCance's Hill on the Stewartstown Road. In the fifties no woman felt properly dressed without a string of synthetic pearls. Survivors of the Holocaust established the making of this jewellery in Belfast.

PRONI

BELOW:
Making analogue computer parts at a Short's factory on the Castlereagh Road. New light industries and synthetic fibre plants came into Belfast and its periphery in the late 1950s and provided employment opportunities at a time when traditional engineering and linen manufacture were in decline. Despite an apparently encouraging start, however, Belfast was not to become a leading centre in the information technology revolution.

PRONI

RIGHT:
Dr Harold Love with Nurse Helen Smyth
anaesthetise a young outpatient prior to a dental
extraction at the children's hospital.

ROYAL BELFAST HOSPITAL FOR SICK CHILDREN

BELOW:
Women queuing for polio vaccinations at
lunchtime in 1959. By the end of the decade 12
per cent of the city's rates were being assigned to
public health, though the bulk of expenditure
came from general taxation supported by
subventions from the national exchequer. The
1950s saw perhaps the most striking improvement
in the health of citizens in the century. The old
dispensaries and voluntary institutions were
replaced by the Northern Ireland Hospitals
Authority and services centrally administered by
the General Health Services Board. By 1948 there
were 46 outpatients departments in Belfast and by
1959 these had risen to 85. The campaign to
eliminate tuberculosis achieved rapid success; polio
took longer to eliminate but the blanket
administration of a vaccine eventually wiped out
this crippling and often killing disease.

PRONI

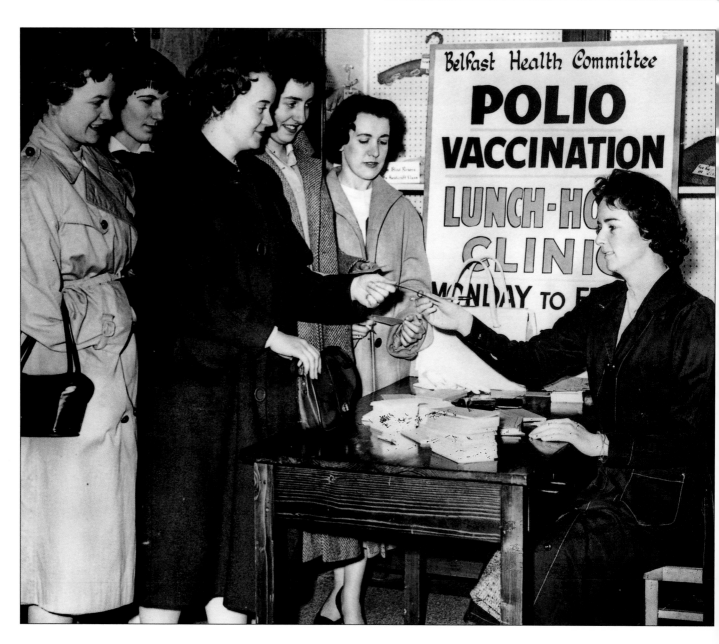

LEFT:
Harrison's hardware shop on the Albertbridge Road, typical of many such stores that continued to flourish in the city before more widespread use of the motor car allowed large centralised warehouses to emerge. The former owner of these premises was the maternal grandmother of St John Ervine (1883–1971), biographer, novelist and playwright, who lived here as a child. Significantly, his best-known play was *Boyd's Shop* which played to capacity audiences in the Group Theatre in Bedford Street in the 1940s; the novelist Sam Hanna Bell observed: 'Some quality in St John Ervine's play reminded men and women of homely virtues reported missing if not dead in those sombre early days and black nights of the War.'

BBC NI

BELOW:
Eason and Son in Great Victoria Street railway station in 1956. The advertisements and posters indicate that the reading public was not obsessed merely with local issues. Broader themes, such as the pros and cons of capital punishment, seem to dominate in this year of the Suez crisis and the Hungarian revolution.

EASON & SON NI

RIGHT:
'Young Francis' McPeake (1917–1986), founder of the McPeake Trio, who went on to win the Llangollen International Music Eisteddfod three times. His own children later joined, raising the number in the group to six, and established the Clonard Traditional Music School. His father, also called Francis and a member of the group, was one of the greatest exponents of the art of playing uilleann pipes, an art then in grave danger of being lost. The McPeakes enjoyed enormous popularity during the traditional music revival of the late 1950s and early 1960s. In this photograph Francis McPeake takes part in the Northern Ireland Home Service programme *Accent on Melody* in December 1954.

BBC NI

BELOW:
Stanley Wyllie, whose name was familiar to almost everyone in Belfast in the fifties, playing the incomparable Compton organ at the Ritz cinema in 1954.

BBC NI

The Belfast Empire Theatre of Varieties in Victoria Square. There was a fire station here between 1850 and 1870 and around 1864 the Colosseum Music Hall opened at number 16, becoming the Buffalo Hotel and Music Hall in 1881. Rebuilt as the Empire in 1894 to a design by J.J. Farrell, it attracted all the leading music-hall stars of the day, including Marie Lloyd, Little Titch, Harry Lauder, George Formby and Gertie Gitana, and the first theatre broadcast in Northern Ireland was made from here in 1937. Though still popular and much loved in the 1950s, the theatre was not paying its way. At the end of the decade the Empire closed and the building – described by architectural historian Marcus Patton as 'a splendid confection of Venetian polychrome brickwork with stripey ogee arches and frilly overhanging eaves' – was pulled down.

BBC NI

RIGHT

John Luke (1906–75) at work on a large mural in the dome of the City Hall,
commissioned to commemorate the Festival of Britain in 1951. After an
elementary education at Hillman Street National School, Luke began work as
a riveter's boy in the shipyard and later worked in the York Street mill. He
attended evening classes in art and won a scholarship to study at the Slade
School of Art in London. He returned to Belfast in 1931 and developed his
own unique style, representing landscapes in County Armagh and the west
and industrial Belfast, a city of which he was inordinately proud.

BBC N

BELOW

A viewing at Basil Blackshaw's exhibition at the CEMA gallery, January
1956. In 1955 Blackshaw was the youngest artist to have been recognised
with a one-man show in Belfast, organised by John Hewitt, Keeper of Art
and Deputy Director of the Belfast Museum and Art Gallery. Born in 1932
Blackshaw was one of an exceptionally talented group of students trained at
the Belfast College of Art after the Second World War and admirers found
in his paintings of landscapes, horses and disturbing figure studies the
influences of Cézanne and Mark Rothko.

PRON

LEFT:
Olive Henry, born in 1902 and educated at Mountpottinger National School and Victoria College, became Belfast's most admired artist in stained glass. After attending evening classes at the Belfast School of Art, she became an apprentice in the firm of W.F. Clokey and Company in King Street in 1919 and remained there for the rest of her working life until 1972. She was a regular exhibitor in Belfast from 1928 and had her own one-woman show in the CEMA gallery in Donegall Place in 1957. Her paintings were representational but because pattern and shape attracted her, they at first glance appeared abstract.

BBC NI

Ruby Murray, certainly the most famous Belfast citizen in the 1950s. She began her singing career with the choir of Richmond Presbyterian Church on the Donegall Road and went on to top the hit parade several times. She had a very distinctive sweet voice and a special 'girl-next-door' appeal. For many no song better evokes this decade than her rendition of 'Softly, Softly'.

BBC NI

The Harmony Hawaiians, one of many groups formed in the city as the world of popular music was being transformed by stronger transatlantic influences, the advent of rock music and stars such as Chuck Berry, Lonnie Donegan and Elvis Presley.

BBC NI

ABOVE:
The Spring Fashion Show at Robb's in High Street. This was the era of the department store and the leading ones in Belfast were Robinson and Cleaver's, Anderson and McAuley's, Brands and Norman's, the Bank Buildings, the Belfast Co-operative in York Street and Robb's.

PRONI

LEFT:
The Bell family from north Belfast meet Santa at the Belfast Royal Antedeluvian Order of Buffaloes Christmas party in 1954. A visit to Father Christmas was a magical experience and Santa's grotto – in the Co-op or in Robb's – was always a popular destination.

BELL FAMILY

1960s

ON 16 MARCH 1960 THE PEOPLE OF BELFAST gathered to witness the launch of the 45,000-ton P & O liner *Canberra*. This was the last great launching of its kind in Belfast – the growing success of air transport had severely curtailed the demand for this type of large passenger vessel that had made the reputation of Harland and Wolff, and competition from the Far East and elsewhere had become more intense. The work force in the shipyards fell from 20,000 to 13,000 and, while the firm became a noted builder of large oil tankers, the great days when the 'yard' held a pivotal position in the city's economy were passing away.

The decade began with gloomy prognostications for the city's economic future as the demand for Belfast's traditional export industries slackened. Linen had still been the main employer of labour in Belfast ten years earlier; now facing competition from synthetic fibres and cotton, the flax mills which for so long had dominated the city's skyline closed one by one.

As it turned out, the world economy enjoyed an unprecedented boom in the 1960s and the

OPPOSITE:
Smithfield 1960: This partly covered market drew customers from all over the city in search of second-hand books, Victorian prints, old jewellery, furniture old and new, pets, goldfish, and musical instruments. Struggling artists often came here in search of inexpensive frames for their paintings and collectors always hoped that, amongst the bric-à-brac, they would come upon a genuine antique. The most famous shops were owned by the bookseller Harry Hall, who specialised in rare maps, and Joseph Kavanagh who had the words 'I Buy Anything' prominently displayed.

KENNETH McNALLY

RIGHT:
Van Morrison and Them, psyching up to appear on *Ready Steady Go* in 1964, a performance that did much to launch Van Morrison's career. Other members of the group were Pat McAuley, Alan Henderson, Billy Harrison, and John McAuley. They launched themselves with an unrestrained version of Slim Harpo's 'Don't Start Crying Now' and attracted a devoted following in venues such as the Plaza and the Maritime Hotel in College Square North.

MONITOR PRESS

Stormont government was highly successful in attracting multinational firms to set up
factories in Northern Ireland, including Belfast and its periphery. In
addition, while businesses such as the ropeworks and Musgrave's went to
the wall, several long-established firms modernised and increased their
sales, including Mackie's, the Sirocco Works, Short's, and Gallaher's. Helped
by growing subsidies from the central exchequer, public employment
increased, living standards rose rapidly and the expansion of the National
Health Service and of educational facilities left an impression of continuous
progress.

The ferocity of the Divis Street riots in 1964 demonstrated that ancient
divisions had not been spirited away by growing prosperity. Nevertheless,
many trusted that the appointment of Captain Terence O'Neill as prime
minister in 1963 would result in an easing of tensions and the visit to
Stormont of Taoiseach Sean Lemass in January 1965 seemed to usher in a
new era. To many loyalists, however, O'Neill was conceding too much in
his programme of reconciliation, while Catholics became intensely
frustrated by his failure to implement real reforms and to ensure fairness in
public appointments and in the allocation of council houses. In 1966
feelings ran high during the fiftieth anniversary commemorations of the
1916 rising, over the naming of a new bridge over the Lagan during
demonstrations organised by the moderator of the Free Presbyterian
Church, the Reverend Ian Paisley, and when three Catholics were shot in
Malvern Street in June and Peter Ward died of his wounds. The decade
ended in tragedy as intense riots convulsed much of the city and, following
the Battle of the Bogside in Derry in August 1969, people were burned
out of their homes, barricades were erected, troops patrolled the streets on
active service and the first violent deaths occurred in what was to be more
than a quarter-century of the Troubles.

Phase one of the M2, opened in October 1966. Ireland's first motorway, the M1, had opened in 1962 and initially ran from Belfast to Lisburn, subsequently being extended to Dungannon. The M2 headed in a northern and north-westerly direction, easing traffic to and from Derry and Coleraine/Ballymena. The one-and-a-half-mile section between Whitla Street and Greencastle was built on the soft mud of the foreshore using 4 million tons of basalt brought in by rail from Magheramorne – the last commercial use of steam locomotives in Northern Ireland. The M2 rapidly became the most heavily used road in the region and by 1988 it was carrying an average of 70,000 vehicles a day. Alarmed at the spiralling cost of motorway construction, the British government attempted to curtail this project in 1964 but it was saved when Prime Minister Terence O'Neill travelled to London to argue its case with Prime Minister Sir Alec Douglas-Home.

PRONI

Early 1963 brought the 'big snow' to Belfast, with almost unbelievable conditions of snow, ice and gales – followed by the misery of ankle-deep slush as the snow thawed.

BBC NI

BELOW
East Belfast was poorly provided with public
open spaces and Victoria Park with its boating
lake was always well used

LINEN HALL LIBRARY

BELOW:
The launch of the *Canberra* at
Harland and Wolff on 16 March
1960. This vessel was built
primarily to carry emigrants to
the southern hemisphere; many
people from Belfast responded
to the government offer of the
£10 passage to make new lives
for themselves in Australia.
Harland and Wolff was still the
largest shipbuilding unit in the
world; its works covered 300
acres and employed 20,000
workers. *Canberra*, however, was
the last great liner to be
launched in Belfast and, facing a
fall in world shipping freight
rates and stiffer international
competition, the famous firm
suffered from a shortage of
orders and the workforce fell to
around 13,000.

BELFAST TELEGRAPH

LEFT:
The Short's Skyvan over New York. Orders for sixty-seven of these versatile light freighters had been won by 1967. This was the real success of Short's in this decade after a period during which much of the firm's highly advanced research and development had failed to yield a significant commercial return.

BOMBARDIER AEROSPACE

BELOW:
The Sea Quest oil rig being towed from the shipyard into Belfast Lough in January 1966, the first time that such a structure had been launched complete. The construction of this oil rig of American design was an impressive technical achievement but there were no further orders and in June accountants Price Waterhouse ominously reported that Harland and Wolff was 'unable to put its financial house in order from its own internal resources'.

BILL KIRK

RIGHT:
The open toastrack bus, which ran from the Antrim Road up through Hazelwood to the plateau at the entrance of Bellevue Zoo, was a favourite treat for children.

BELFAST CITY COUNCIL

BELOW:
The winning team from the Royal Belfast Academical Institution on the *Top of the Form* competition on BBC television in 1963. 'Inst' was founded in 1810 by a group of Presbyterians, led by the founder of the United Irishmen, Dr William Drennan. Intended to be a Belfast equivalent of dissenting academies in Scotland, it had a medical school and awarded degrees until the setting up of Queen's College in 1849. Its teachers had a reputation for being too liberal for the majority of Presbyterians in Belfast.

BBC NI

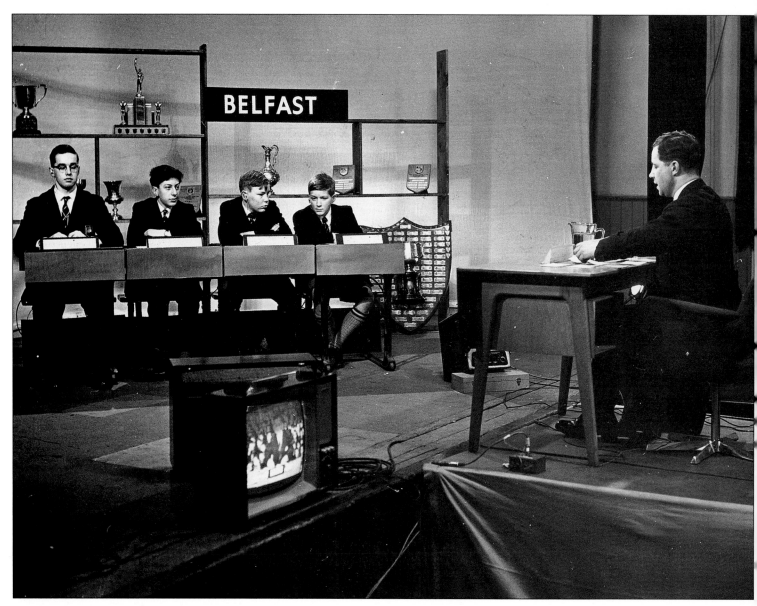

LEFT:
Popularly known as the 'Cooler', this pool in the Falls Park was extremely busy in hot weather. So dense was the population in this part of the city, and such was the popularity of the 'cooler', that it was not possible to walk round the pool on some summer days. Anxieties about hygiene, and the danger of swimmers contracting polio in particular, led to the closure of the pool by the end of the decade.

BELFAST CITY COUNCIL

BELOW:
Constructing the annual bonfire in Sandy Row, July 1964. The IRA border campaign had been called off and intercommunal tensions had apparently eased so much that the bonfires of the Eleventh night began to attract people from the suburbs with little or no interest in celebrating the seventeenth-century triumphs of King William.

LINEN HALL LIBRARY

RIGHT:
The Variety Market in 1960. Held every Friday, it was not only a boisterous and colourful addition to Belfast life but a great place to buy cheap food and second-hand goods.

KENNETH McNALLY

BELOW:
This view of Carrick Hill Place, off Peter's Hill, in 1961 shows dilapidated nineteenth-century housing in urgent need of replacement. In 1945 William Grant, the former shipyard worker who became minister of health and local government, set himself a target of building 100,000 local authority houses, most of them in Belfast, and this goal was finally reached in the early 1960s. Nevertheless, the city's housing problem remained formidable: the rate of house building by Belfast Corporation, the Northern Ireland Housing Trust and subsidised private builders had been sufficient only to keep pace with the increase in the number of new households. In 1962 the city architect reported that 58,700 new dwellings would be required over the next twenty years.

KENNETH McNALLY

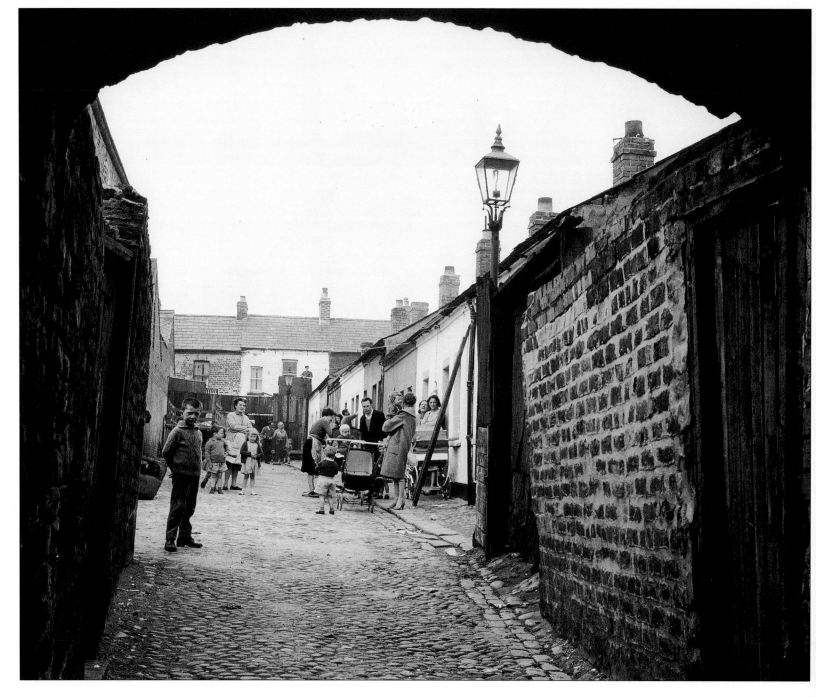

LEFT:

The office of the Irish Republican candidate, Liam McMillan, in Divis Street during the Westminster general election campaign of 1964. When the Reverend Ian Paisley learned that an Irish tricolour was on display in the window, he threatened to take his supporters there to remove it if the authorities did not act. The RUC removed the flag but clashed with local people. Another tricolour appeared and this time the police smashed into the premises with pick axes and removed it. The ensuing rioting was intense: police were driven back by a barrage of stones, scrap metal and bottles; some petrol bombs were thrown; water cannon were used for the first time in more than forty years. It was remarkable that no lives were lost. The violence was limited to a few streets and was quickly over.

BELFAST TELEGRAPH

BELOW:

The Divis Flats complex of twelve medium-rise blocks and one multi-storey tower was begun in 1966 and completed in 1972. The flats were welcomed by the Catholic Church because they retained the local community within St Peter's parish. At the start of the Troubles the roof of the tower was occupied by members of the Irish Republican Socialist Party and acquired the nickname 'Planet of the IRPS'. The British Army later established a fortified base on the same roof, bristling with electronic equipment.

NI HOUSING EXECUTIVE

134

RIGHT:
The famous handshake: Sean Lemass meets Captain Terence O'Neill at Stormont on 14 January 1965. Since he had become taoiseach in 1959, Lemass had been seeking better relations with Britain to promote his economic strategy, and that included a *rapprochement* with Northern Ireland. O'Neill was the first prime minister to make improved community relations a central plank of his programme and he was determined to improve communications with Dublin. For both premiers this meeting involved many political risks and O'Neill did not inform his cabinet colleagues until that morning. 'I shall get into terrible trouble for this' were the first words the taoiseach spoke to the prime minister but in fact no widespread hostile reaction greeted the O'Neill–Lemass meeting.

PRONI

BELOW:
Terence O'Neill behind the cameras at Broadcasting House in Ormeau Avenue. By the end of the sixties circumstances had forced the prime minister to show a more sombre countenance in front of the camera.

BBC NI

Gerry Fitt, the Republican Labour MP for the Stormont constituency of Dock since 1962. He demonstrated formidable skill by getting himself elected for West Belfast in 1966 and the impact he made at Westminster was immediate. This colourful, fast-talking ex-sailor, whose pithy style contrasted with that of the somewhat sedate upper-middle-class Unionists, explained Catholic grievances in terms everyone could understand.

BBC NI

Nationalist Austin Currie (right) and Ulster Unionist John Taylor appearing on BBC NI's *Ulster Opinion*, 1967. Currie leaped to prominence in June 1968 when he gave his backing to local people challenging the allocation of a house in Caledon, County Tyrone, to a single Protestant woman aged nineteen. Currie squatted in the house himself before being removed by a policeman, who happened to be the woman's brother. This incident was a pivotal event in the launch of the civil rights movement.

BBC NI

The Reverend Ian Paisley, founder and moderator of the Free Presbyterian Church, in a 1966 demonstration to Church House in Fisherwick Place to protest at ecumenical and 'romanising' tendencies in the Presbyterian Church. Paisley, whose main base is now the Martyrs' Memorial Church on the Ravenhill Road, was for long the most vociferous and persistent critic of Terence O'Neill and of his bridge-building gestures to the Catholic minority.

BELFAST TELEGRAPH

A horse being watered at Donegall Quay in 1960. Working horses remained a familiar feature of Belfast streets in the 1960s and were particularly favoured for carting sacks of coal and coke, and for making deliveries. Water troughs were to be found all over the city, some erected as memorials, and horses would stand eating oats from nosebags, surrounded by sparrows ready to pick up falling grains.

KENNETH McNALLY

LEFT:
Trolley buses, first introduced on the Falls Road in 1938, were more versatile than trams and had a greater range. By the end of the 1960s, however, they had been entirely replaced by diesel-driven buses.

BELFAST TELEGRAPH

BELOW:
Smithfield Market in its heyday, 1960. The Smithfield area was the nucleus of Catholic west Belfast where the first power-driven cotton mills had been built towards the end of the eighteenth century and a colourful market developed here from the outset. Thomas Gaffikin described Smithfield as he remembered it in the 1820s: 'Many people resorted to Smithfield on Friday evenings to witness the different spectacles and amusements provided by the grinning clowns at the show booths, and the recruiting parties playing the "British Grenadiers" with fife and drum . . . the hum of voices, the bargaining for knacker's horses, the shouting of the cheap jacks, all combined to enliven the scene.' By the 1960s the recruiting parties, clowns and horses had long gone but Smithfield was still a lively place to look for a bargain.

KENNETH McNALLY

ABOVE LEFT:
Colin Middleton (1910–83), painter. Born in Belfast, he was educated at Belfast Royal Academy and was then apprenticed as a damask designer and studied part-time at the Belfast College of Art. He spent most of his life as a teacher in Belfast, Coleraine and Lisburn until the Arts Council of Northern Ireland awarded him funding which allowed him to paint full-time. He had a one-man show at the Belfast Museum and Art Gallery in 1943 and was a member of the Royal Ulster Academy and the Royal Hibernian Academy.

BBC NI

ABOVE RIGHT:
Gerard Dillon (1916–71), painter, designer and graphic artist. Born in west Belfast, he was educated at Raglan Street School, and by the Christian Brothers and was apprenticed to a house painter in 1930. After attending the Belfast College of Art, he painted in London, Dublin and Connemara. His first major exhibition was in 1943 and for a time he designed sets, posters and costumes for the Abbey Theatre.

BBC NI

The Shaftesbury Square branch of the Ulster Bank, opened in 1964 Elizabeth Frink's aluminium *Airborne Men* caused much controversy – most people in Belfast were either bemused or critical and referred to this sculpture on the gable wall as 'the angels'

ULSTER BANK

LEFT:
Mary O'Malley, founder of the Lyric Theatre.
Concerned at the lack of opportunity to stage
serious plays in Belfast, she and her husband
Pearse converted part of their home in
Derryvolgie Avenue into a theatre, and a
succession of productions by W.B. Yeats,
Bertold Brecht, Samuel Beckett, Arthur Miller
and others gave people in the city the chance
to see live international drama, often for the
first time. The Lyric moved in 1968 to a
handsome new theatre in Ridgeway Street.

BBC NI

Helen Lewis (right)
rehearsing with dancers
Emma Kennedy and Hugh
Murray. Born in Trutnov,
Czechoslovakia, she trained at
Milca Mayerová's School of
Dance in Prague but in 1942
she was deported to the
Jewish ghetto of Terezín and
then to Auschwitz. The fitness
she acquired before the war
helped her to survive the
horrors of the death camp
and the terrible journey from
Lauenburg on the Baltic back
to Prague. She married Harry
Lewis in 1947 and he took
her to Belfast where she still
lives. She began to
choreograph in theatre and
opera, and her teaching
eventually led to the
foundation of the Belfast
Modern Dance Group.

HELEN LEWIS

RIGHT:
James Ellis was well known in the city as an actor in the Group Theatre before he became a star of the immensely popular television series, *Z Cars*, making the Belfast accent familiar to British viewers for the first time in his character of Bert Lynch.

BBC NI

BELOW:
The Long and the Short and the Tall at the Arts Theatre, 1963. The theatre started life as the Mask Theatre in Linenhall Street, founded by Hubert Wilmot in 1944, and opened with *The Flashing Stream*. When American troops took over the premises it moved to an attic in Upper North Street and, in 1954, to a disused auction room in Little Donegall Street. It found a permanent home in Botanic Avenue in 1961, the first playhouse to be built in Belfast for fifty years. Its first performance there was Tennessee Williams's *Orpheus Descending*. Wilmot gave Belfast theatre goers the opportunity to see a wide range of international plays by Ionescu, Gazzo, Bolt and others and put on the first production of the stage adaptation of Arthur Koestler's *Darkness at Noon* outside the United States. Actors including Maurice O'Callaghan, Doreen Hepburn, Harry Towb and Catherine Gibson launched their careers under Wilmot's direction. To attract larger audiences, the variety of productions was broadened and a series of farces by Sam Cree proved especially popular. Belfast City Council gave vital support but competition from other venues proved too much and the theatre closed in the late 1990s.

KENNETH McNALLY

LEFT:
James Young stirs the Christmas pudding on board HMS *Maidstone* in 1969. Young was by far the most gifted and popular comedian in Belfast. His acting career began when he took the part of George in Steinbeck's *Of Mice and Men* at the Group Theatre and played Derek, the window cleaner, in the radio series *The McCooeys*. He could adopt to perfection the part of many Belfast characters, his portrayal of children and of the *nouveau riche* Cherryvalley lady being especially memorable. He was manager of the Group Theatre between 1960 and 1972 and had his own television programme shortly before his death in 1974.

BELFAST TELEGRAPH

ABOVE:
Ulster Television's popular children's series *Romper Room*, with presenter Miss Adrienne and two of her 'do bes'. This station – better known simply as UTV – began broadcasting in 1959, with studios at Havelock House, a former linen warehouse on the Ormeau Road.

KENNETH McNALLY

LEFT:
UTV's *Teatime with Tommy*: Tommy James played requests for local viewers.

St Patrick's Night in the Ulster Hall, 1969, with the BBC Northern Ireland Orchestra conducted by Edgar Boucher. Designed by W. J. Barre, this was one of the largest halls in the United Kingdom when it opened in 1862. Until the completion of the Waterfront Hall in the 1990s it was Belfast's principal concert hall and was used for political rallies and meetings, religious services, pop concerts, orchestral performances and boxing matches. The hall annexed to it is the home of the Group Theatre. The massive Victorian Mulholland organ towers over the stage.

BBC NI

The Plattermen, one of the most prestigious and best-loved showbands in the country. Professional musicians referred to them as 'The Heads' because they were regarded as the finest players in their field. The city's most prominent promoter, Jim Aiken, was certain of a packed dance hall when he booked the band to appear on Tuesday nights in the Orpheus.

BBC NI

Ballroom dancing in the Plaza in Chichester Street. The Plaza was for long one of the city's great social institutions: in the 1930s mothers brought their marriageable daughters (who had previously been given dance lessons) to afternoon dances here, while they drank tea at tables under the balcony; during the Second World War, after being damaged during the blitz, the dance hall reopened to become a favourite resort for American servicemen and big bands, to the delight of local girls and the chagrin of young men who were often refused entry when GIs were there in force. In the post-war years it was immensely popular not only in the evenings and afternoons but also in the middle of the day when office and factory workers used their lunch breaks to perfect their foxtrots, quicksteps and the twist. With the advent of rock music and discos, this era was drawing to a close in the 1960s.

BBC NI

Teenagers queuing for Rolling Stones concert tickets, 1965.

BELFAST TELEGRAPH

The Pretty Things played at the Plaza on 2 August 1966, when their hit 'A House in the Country' was in the charts.

BELFAST TELEGRAPH

The youth of Belfast were determined that the place should be a swinging city and gave rapturous receptions to the leading groups of the day. The Beatles appeared at the ABC Cinema in November 1963 and it was reported that the teenage population had broken out 'in almost unbelievable scenes of mass hysteria'. The disorder greeting Mick Jagger and the Rolling Stones in the Ulster Hall on 31 July 1964 'made the Beatles look like Old Time Music Hall', according to the *Belfast Telegraph* report, which continues: 'The fans were fainting like nine-pins. They were screaming, hysterical and some of them troublesome. Some had to be strapped to stretchers. And were they the riff-raff of Ulster teenage society? Not at all. They were well-brought-up grammar school girls – nearly a hundred fainted during the madhouse performance. . .'

Hysterical fans are helped off the stage by St John Ambulance personnel as the Rolling Stones make their appearance at the Ulster Hall, 14 August 1965.

BELFAST TELEGRAPH

Hippies from San Francisco, in Botanic Gardens, bring flower power to Northern Ireland. Such visitors were especially exotic because Belfast then attracted only a sprinkling of tourists. In 1969, and for many years afterwards, hotels and guesthouses filled their rooms largely with foreign journalists stationed in Belfast to report the Troubles.

BELFAST TELEGRAPH

Harry Thompson (in the foreground) as the anchor man, with W.D. Flackes and Michael Baguley, in a BBC studio covering the Northern Ireland general election held on 24 February 1969. This was one of the most confused electoral contests in Northern Ireland's history. It was called because Prime Minister Terence O'Neill was challenged from within his party by members who felt he was being too conciliatory to the Catholic minority: the previous month Brian Faulkner and William Morgan had resigned from the cabinet and twelve Unionist MPs had met in Portadown, County Armagh, on 3 February and called for O'Neill's resignation. O'Neill, in retrospect, fared quite well in the election but his position became increasingly untenable and after a series of loyalist bomb attacks he resigned on 28 April 1969.

BBC NI

Kevin Boyle, later a professor of law and political writer, addressing students in Linenhall Street. Four days after the civil rights march in Derry on 5 October 1968, when police batoned unarmed demonstrators before television cameras, some 3,000 students and 20 academic staff from Queen's University set out from Elmwood Avenue towards the City Hall. The marchers accepted police redirection because Ian Paisley had called a meeting on their route at Shaftesbury Square, provided they could proceed to the front of the City Hall. However, some loyalist counter-demonstrators reached the city centre before them, and the RUC stopped the legal march in Linenhall Street where the students held a peaceful sit-down protest. On their return to the university the students formed the People's Democracy.

VICTOR PATTERSON ARCHIVE/
LINEN HALL LIBRARY

Civil rights march setting out from the City Hall to march to Derry on New Year's Day 1969. As the marchers left Belfast they were outnumbered by loyalists led by Major Ronald Bunting (second from left) who promised to 'harry and harass' the march all the way to Derry. It was the fateful assault on the marchers at Burntollet that precipitated communal violence, leading to the first deaths of the Troubles in August 1969.

BELFAST TELEGRAPH

Anti-Vietnam War protesters lie in the path of members of the crew of the USS *Keppler* taking part in the Lord Mayor's Show on 18 May 1968. The storm of popular protest which swept American cities and campuses, Paris, Prague, London and other places, was reduced to a gentle ripple when it reached Belfast that spring. By the late autumn, however, demonstrations, marches and riots were beginning to draw the city to the attention of foreign journalists.

BELFAST TELEGRAPH

ABOVE:

Lower Falls, Friday 15 August 1969: the British Army arrives on the streets of Belfast. The decision
to bring in the troops was made after the Battle of the Bogside in Derry, when Catholics clashed
with the police after an Apprentice Boys parade on 12 August. There had been intense rioting in
Belfast on 14 August, followed by general gunfire as darkness fell: six people were killed or mortally
wounded, including a nine-year-old boy killed in Divis Flats by a police machine-gun bullet as he
took refuge in his bedroom. Residents on the Falls Road, preferring soldiers to armed police, plied
them with cups of tea. Not enough troops had been brought in to prevent further violence that
night: virtually all the houses in Bombay Street in Clonard were destroyed; other houses in
Brookfield were set on fire; and a Protestant rioter was killed in Ardoyne.

BELFAST TELEGRAPH

OPPOSITE TOP:

Shankill Road, Saturday 11 October 1969. Around 10 p.m. some 3,000 loyalists advanced towards
Unity Flats and fired on police attempting to halt them, mortally wounding Constable Victor
Arbuckle – the first policeman to be killed in the Troubles. The 3rd Battalion the Light Infantry
moved in and the troops came under protracted rifle and automatic fire and were showered with
petrol bombs. The army fired only twenty-six shots, killing two rioters with cool deliberation.
Loyalist anger had been aroused by the publication the previous day of Lord Hunt's
recommendations on policing, which included the disbandment of the B Specials
and the disarming of the RUC.

BELFAST TELEGRAPH

RIGHT:

Police confront rioters in Hooker Street. At the beginning of August 1969 this was the most violent
point in Northern Ireland: on Saturday 2 August Protestants from Disraeli Street crossed the
Crumlin Road and clashed with Catholics in Hooker Street, forcing people out of their homes and
throwing stones and petrol bombs at the police when they intervened. The following night the
residents of Hooker Street prepared a trench and barricades to keep out invaders, but it was the RUC
which repelled a Protestant crowd. And on Monday Protestants assembled at the end of Disraeli
Street, beating drums and chanting, and again the police repelled them from Hooker Street
but injured a Catholic youth with a Land Rover.

BELFAST TELEGRAPH

1970s

City Centre ➤
Docks

A 300-pound car-bomb blast severely
damages the headquarters of the Northern
Ireland Housing Executive at Fisherwick
Place on 9 November 1972. Facing the
building is the 'Black Man', a bronze statue
of the Reverend Henry Cooke, the founder
of Ulster unionism in the mid-nineteenth
century. The Northern Ireland Housing
Executive was set up in 1971 as a central
agency, taking over functions previously
exercised by local authorities, to build
homes paid for by public funds.

NI HOUSING EXECUTIVE

Petrol bombs were frequently used against the police and British troops, especially in the early stages of the Troubles. The effectiveness of these home-made weapons was first demonstrated at Rossville Flats in Derry: during the three-day Battle of the Bogside in August 1969 one dairy alone lost 43,000 milk bottles.

IRISH NEWS

THIS DECADE WAS THE MOST CONTINUOUSLY VIOLENT one in Belfast's history. Inflamed by fears and clashing aspirations, the community turned in on itself and threatened to reduce the city to a wasteland. British troops, brought in during the bloodshed of August 1969, were on constant active service on the streets; the Provisional IRA and other militant republicans launched a sustained campaign to dislocate the economy and make the region ungovernable; and militant loyalists inflicted murders and assaults on their fellow citizens.

The imposition of internment in August 1971 was followed by unprecedented bloodletting and dislocation. In just three weeks, more than one in every hundred families in Belfast were forced to move as a result of intimidation, fear of intimidation or the destruction of their homes. It was the biggest enforced movement of population in Europe since 1945 and until the eruption of ethnic conflict in the Balkans in the 1990s. In the spring of 1972, fifty-one years of devolved government in Belfast was brought to an end and soon afterwards the corporation was replaced by Belfast City Council, elected by proportional representation. Many of Belfast's Victorian and Edwardian buildings fell easy prey to incendiaries and explosives, and the city centre was almost deserted after nightfall.

The establishment of a power-sharing administration at Stormont precipitated the loyalist strike of May 1974, which not only brought the city to a standstill but also ended hopes of community government for a long time to come. At the same time the international oil crisis was having a particularly devastating impact on the economy of Greater Belfast and one by one the synthetic fibre plants closed. By the end of the decade the city's economy was in crisis and was heavily dependent on subventions from the central exchequer. By then, however, there was a noticeable reduction in the impact of conflict and destruction on the city's inhabitants.

Women marching from Whiterock and Turf Lodge with food for residents trapped in their houses during the lower Falls curfew, 3–5 July 1970. The area was sealed off for thirty-five hours while troops carried out a rigorous house-to-house search for arms. When volunteers of the Official IRA began shooting, troops fired 1,500 rounds and killed three people, including a press photographer. Another person was crushed to death by an armoured car. Though over one hundred weapons were found, the curfew was a political blunder: the *Sunday Times* Insight Team concluded that 'recruitment to the Provisionals was dizzily fast: the movement grew from fewer than a hundred activists to nearly 800 by December'.

IRISH NEWS

The Provisional IRA make a defiant mark on the Black Mountain overlooking west Belfast. When the Troubles began a Scotland Yard confidential document confirmed that the IRA 'is not organised or equipped to play a significant independent role' within the Northern Ireland Civil Rights Association. In Belfast fewer than sixty men regarded themselves as IRA members and in May 1969 the IRA's total arsenal in the city was a machine gun, a pistol, and some ammunition. By the end of the year a new militant republican organisation, the Provisionals, had emerged.

IRISH NEWS

LEFT:
Women warn of approaching security forces by blowing whistles and banging dustbin lids. Such warnings became common after the introduction of internment. Just after 4 a.m. on Monday 9 August 1971 thousands of soldiers set out in arrest squads, each accompanied by an RUC Special Branch officer, to identify terrorist suspects. The internment operation was completed by 7.30 a.m. and many of the 342 men seized were transferred either to Crumlin Road jail or to the *Maidstone*, a prison ship moored in Belfast Lough.

IRISH NEWS

BELOW:
Farringdon Gardens, August 1971. In this street and in Velsheda Park and Cranbrook Park in Ardoyne about 240 houses were destroyed by fire. The most violent day since 1969, eleven people were killed in Belfast alone, including Father Hugh Mullan, shot while administering the last rites to an injured man in Ballymurphy.

PA NEWS

Following the imposition of internment, the Provisional IRA intensified its campaign. The Four Step Inn on the Shankill Road, 29 September 1971. The bomb planted here by the IRA killed 2 people and injured 20. Other atrocities of this time include a bomb at the Northern Ireland Electricity Board's central office, which killed 1 person and maimed 16 others; and the bombing of the Red Lion restaurant on the Ormeau Road on 2 November, which killed 3 people and left 36 injured.

BELFAST TELEGRAPH

McGurk's public house in North Queen Street, bombed on 4 December 1971. This was the most horrific single incident of the Troubles in Belfast. Fifteen people were killed; by the light of arc lamps surgeons treated the injured in the open; gas escaping from fractured pipes flamed in the rubble as all through the night the dead and mutilated were uncovered brick by brick; and rescue operations were hampered as nearby the army came under fire and rival crowds fought in the darkness. The bomb had been planted by loyalist paramilitaries.

BELFAST TELEGRAPH

The Abercorn restaurant in Castle Lane, bombed by the Provisional IRA when it was crowded with shoppers on Saturday 4 March 1972. Janet Bereen and Anne Owens had been sitting almost on top of the bomb when it exploded. They were killed. Four people lost both legs and at least 136 people were injured, many of them very severely.

BELFAST TELEGRAPH

Bloody Friday, 21 July 1972. The day began with a 21-year-old Catholic being murdered when he answered a knock to his door in the Springfield area. At 2.10 p.m. a large bomb exploded at the Smithfield bus depot, destroying 30 buses; at 2.16 p.m. the Brookvale Hotel off the Antrim Road was demolished with a suitcase bomb; 7 minutes later a bomb placed on a platform at York Road railway station blew off the roof; and at 2.45 p.m. a car bomb at Star Taxis on the Crumlin Road wrecked nearby tax offices. Between 2.48 p.m. and 3.12 p.m. 13 more explosions reverberated in and around Belfast. In the worst atrocities of this IRA bomb blitz, 6 people were killed at Oxford Street bus station and at the Cavehill Road shopping centre a bomb in a hijacked vehicle exploded without warning, killing 3 people including a mother of 7 children. Altogether 9 people had been killed and at least 130 maimed by blasts in the city. Four more people died violently in Belfast as night closed in.

BELFAST TELEGRAPH

Security gates at Castle Lane, 1973. One government response to the sustained IRA bombing campaign was to erect barriers round the city centre. Everyone coming through the barriers had to be searched. All the main stores also had their own security checks.

BILL KIRK

British soldiers try to make themselves comfortable in Skipper Street in 1972. Troops brought into Belfast in 1969 could not have foretold that they would remain on active service on the streets for almost three decades.

BILL KIRK

LEFT:
Security forces searching for arms in the Markets in 1974. Since it was possible to stow an Armalite rifle in a cereal packet, the movement of terrorist weapons presented the security forces with acute problems in the 1970s as searches could accentuate the alienation of local people.

BELFAST TELEGRAPH

BELOW:
21 December 1972: smoke pours out of wrecked shops in Donegall Street in the city centre, which was evacuated by soldiers and police after a Christmas shopper had spotted an abandoned car. Minutes later the explosion occurred.

EASON & SON, NI

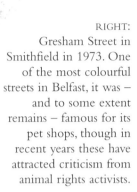

RIGHT:
Gresham Street in
Smithfield in 1973. One
of the most colourful
streets in Belfast, it was –
and to some extent
remains – famous for its
pet shops, though in
recent years these have
attracted criticism from
animal rights activists.

BILL KIRK

BELOW:
Klondyke Bar,
Sandy Row, 1972.

BILL KIRK

LEFT:

George Best, at his peak described by the legendary Pelé as the best footballer in the world. Brought up in Donard Street and the Cregagh estate, and educated at Lisnasharragh Secondary School, he began his professional career in England at the age of fifteen (suffering from homesickness, he returned to Belfast after the first day and was persuaded to go back only with great difficulty). He kicked his first goal for Manchester United on his second appearance for the club in December 1963 and before his eighteenth birthday he had scored six first-team goals. He was also responsible for two out of the five goals that secured United's victory over Benfica in the European Cup quarter-finals in March 1966. He found it difficult to cope with being an international celebrity, however, and his career declined rapidly thereafter.

BELFAST TELEGRAPH

BELOW:

Mary Peters, with her trainer Buster McShane, acknowledging a warm reception in Royal Avenue after winning a gold medal for the pentathlon and setting a new world record at the Olympic Games in Munich in 1972. Born in Liverpool, she became a teacher in Graymount Girls' Secondary School after qualifying from the Belfast College of Domestic Science. As well as serving several terms as Northern Ireland team manager, she became very active in public life, her positions including vice-chair of the Sports Council and deputy chair of the Northern Ireland Tourist Board.

BELFAST TELEGRAPH

Delivering milk during the Ulster Workers' Council strike in 1974. On the evening of 14 May 1974 Protestant workers in the power stations and elsewhere began a fifteen-day strike that paralysed most of Northern Ireland. By Saturday 18 May Belfast was experiencing blackouts lasting up to six hours at a time; Tilley lamps hissed on the counters of large department stores; and bakeries were forced to shut down. On Sunday night the UWC ordered the erection of almost one hundred road blocks to encircle central Belfast and the following morning gangs of youths hijacked lorries and cars to seal off most of the main routes into the city.

BILL KIRK

British Army at the Harbour Estate. After Harold Wilson's broadcast on 25 May 1974, when he denounced 'people who spend their lives sponging on Westminster and British democracy', the British Army was ordered to take action. The intervention was limited to a takeover of fuel supplies and the distribution of petrol from a limited number of stations. Civil servants who were supposed to deal with cash and the appropriate number of Green Shield stamps failed to appear. 'We found ourselves doing this,' one army officer remembered. 'We handled the cash and pumped the petrol. I don't expect they ever squared the books since then. But we did the chore they asked us to do!'

BELFAST TELEGRAPH

The Reverend Ian Paisley leading a parade celebrating the collapse of the power-sharing executive. On his left, partly obscured, is Harry West, who had been dismissed by Terence O'Neill as agriculture minister in 1967; on his right is Glenn Barr, chairman of the Ulster Workers' Council; and to Barr's right, under the Union flag, is Bill Craig, leader of Vanguard, a recently formed hard-line unionist party. A controversial broadcast by Prime Minister Harold Wilson on 25 May 1974 had rallied Protestant feeling behind the strikers and in response the UWC had ordered a reduction in electricity to 10 per cent of capacity and a withdrawal of workers in essential services. Brian Faulkner, chief executive of the power-sharing administration, resigned on 27 May.

BELFAST TELEGRAPH

The finale of the loyalist victory parade to mark the success of the Ulster Workers' Council strike in bringing down the power-sharing executive at Stormont. The formation of this devolved government had been agreed in December 1973 at Sunningdale, but loyalists opposed to it immediately started to put up slogans round the city saying 'Dublin is only a Sunningdale away'. In the general election of February 1974, eleven out of Northern Ireland's twelve MPs elected were members of the loyalist pact opposed to the agreement. Prime Minister Harold Wilson visited Belfast on 18 April and declared that there could be no alternative to the executive, but the UWC strike ensured that it would fail.

BELFAST TELEGRAPH

RIGHT:
George Hamilton and Gloria Hunniford launching BBC Radio Ulster in 1975. Gloria Hunniford is one of several local presenters who went on to achieve success in the television networks.

BBC NI

BELOW:
Clubsound, a highly popular cabaret act founded by George Jones. The group combined comedy with smooth, accessible music and played at Las Vegas and other international venues, but was best loved in its native city, particularly for its rendition of a Tommy Thomas song:

Belfast, Belfast, it's a wonderful town,
It doesn't matter if your skin is brown.
Belfast, Belfast, I love you,
If you're out of work you can get the b'roo.

George Jones later hosted his own inimitable late-afternoon programme on BBC Radio Ulster, *Just Jones*, and only he knows the identity of Sadie, the Belfast know-all

BBC NI

LEFT:

On Tuesday 10 August 1976 Anne Maguire and her four children were walking near their home at Finaghy in south Belfast when a wounded gunman's getaway car crashed into them. Mrs Maguire was badly injured, two of her children were killed and a third child died the following day. Next day her sister, Mairead Corrigan (left) and Betty Williams, who had witnessed the tragedy, founded the Peace People. This movement captured the imagination of Northern Ireland people to an extent that other reconciliation groups had not. The two women were jointly awarded the 1976 Nobel Peace Prize but in a deeply divided society, embittered by seven years of violence, the Peace People found it difficult to sustain widespread support in the long term.

BELFAST TELEGRAPH

BELOW:

A Peace People rally at the City Hall to welcome home the winners of the Nobel Peace Prize. On 12 August 1976 over a thousand women had gathered at the spot where the three Maguire children had died, and six thousand people signed a peace petition organised by women in Andersonstown. Two days later several busloads of women from the Shankill joined another peace rally at the same place; twenty thousand attended a peace rally in Ormeau Park; a similar number marched up the Shankill Road a week later; and in the following weeks peace rallies were held all over Northern Ireland, in many places in the south, and in London.

BELFAST TELEGRAPH

The Reverend Ian Paisley stands alone at the gates of Parliament Buildings at Stormont during the 'constitutional stoppage' in May 1977. A Constitutional Convention, elected to search for a political formula for Northern Ireland, had rejected power-sharing in its report in November 1975, and for that reason the Westminster government refused to implement it. Paisley headed an organisation calling itself the United Unionist Action Council, which on 23 April 1977 gave notice to the secretary of state that 'he has seven days to begin a powerful and effective offensive against the IRA and announce steps to implement the Convention Report'. Fearing a repeat of the Ulster Workers' Council strike, the government acted quickly, drafted in more troops and swept away barricades when the 'stoppage' began on 2 May. The power workers failed to join the strike and it quickly collapsed.

PACEMAKER

Queen Elizabeth II visited Belfast in 1977, prompting republicans to organise protest demonstrations. During the latter part of 1976 and throughout 1977 there was a dramatic drop in incidents of political violence: civilian deaths had fallen to 69 in 1977 from 245 in 1976; shootings were down by 33 per cent; explosions by 52 per cent; and there had been no sectarian murders since May 1976.

IRISH NEWS

La Mon House in east Belfast after the firebomb attack of Friday 17 February 1978.
Three experienced Provisionals hooked incendiary bombs onto the security grilles of
this large hotel. It was packed with more than three hundred people attending a variety
of functions, including annual prize distributions by the Northern Ireland Collie Club
and the Northern Ireland Junior Motor Cycle Club. The warning was telephoned too
late and the blasts threw sheets of blazing petrol across a crowded function room.
Twelve people died and twenty-three were horribly injured.

BELFAST TELEGRAPH

168

Leslie Hale in full voice in a marquee tent
A charismatic evangelical preacher, he drew
attendances of thousands but eventually left
Belfast under something of a cloud

BBC N

The grotto of St Mary's Church, Chapel Lane. St Mary's was the first Catholic church in Belfast and was largely paid for by Protestant subscription in 1783. The chapel was rebuilt in 1868 but with the original walls incorporated. A new apse and sacristy were built to designs by Padraig Gregory in 1941. An Italianate arch, with a two-storey tower on one side and a three-storey campanile on the other, were added in 1953.

PRONI

Contralto Bernadette Greevy singing with the choir of St Anne's Church of Ireland Cathedral in 1973. The cathedral had replaced a parish church in Donegall Street, following an appeal for funds by the Archbishop of Canterbury in the Ulster Hall in 1896. The original plans were drawn up by Thomas Drew but it took eight architects and eighty years to complete the cathedral.

BBC NI

Belfast writers (left to right): John Morrow, Ciaran Carson, Frank Ormsby, James Simmons and Michael Longley. Against a bleak background, a vigorous cultural life flourished in the city. It was the 1960s before the full impact of the 1947 Education Act was felt, helping to produce a new crop of talented artists, poets, playwrights and short story writers. In the 1970s writers were encouraged by the founding of two publishing houses, and Queen's University was a focal point, where stimulus and constructive criticism were given by the Queen's Festival and the English Society.

BBC NI

Actor Tom Bell grabs Joe Tomelty during the filming of *The Big Donkey* by Belfast playwright Stewart Love. Tomelty was a prolific writer, an energetic manager and a talented actor who forged links with a new generation of local playwrights who were enjoying increasing success in having their work performed on radio and television.

BBC NI

FAR LEFT:
Barry Douglas, a competitor in Young Musician of the Year, early 1970s. At the age of twenty-six he won the International Tchaikovsky Piano Competition in Moscow in 1986 – the first United Kingdom artist to win this prestigious prize outright. Amongst the many performances which attracted high praise was the concert he gave at the London Proms in 1987: phrases employed by critics included 'immense authority', 'stupendous technique', 'depth of penetration' and 'total commitment'.

BBC NI

LEFT:
Born the son of a butcher in York Road in 1903, James Johnston first attracted attention at the age of fourteen as a member of Jennymount Methodist Choir. He became the most distinguished tenor Belfast ever produced. As principal tenor at Sadler's Wells and Covent Garden between 1945 and 1960 he sang with divas Maria Callas, Joan Sutherland and Victoria de los Angeles.

BBC NI

BELOW:
James Galway, first flautist with the Berlin Philharmonic, 1969–75, talking with composer and arranger Havelock Nelson. Galway learned to play the fife and flute with an Orange band in north Belfast and went on to become one of the most celebrated flautists in the world.

BBC NI

Looking down on Belfast from Cavehill

NI HOUSING EXECUTIVE

1980s

ATRICK BISHOP, WHO WAS the *Observer*'s Ireland correspondent between 1979 and 1982, compared Belfast to 'Berlin after a thousand-bomber raid'. He continued: 'The poverty is ancient and ingrained. The buildings seem to be suffering from a contagion that has covered them with boils and scabs. Single terraces stand in isolation in rubble lakes where bonfires perpetually burn, watched by tough, ragged little boys and skinny dogs. Every surface is etched minutely and obsessively with graffiti.'

Early in 1983 Padraig O'Malley, a political scientist at the University of Massachusetts, described the provincial capital as 'ugly and sore to the eye, the will to go on gone . . . a modern wasteland . . . Only the ghettos have their own vitality. By early evening Belfast is abandoned.' Yet even as these impressions were being written, the transformation of Belfast had begun. The city was extremely tense in 1981 during the hunger strike in the H-Blocks at the Maze prison but, partly as a result of the increase in electoral support for Sinn Féin, the Provisional IRA changed tactics and concentrated on engaging the security forces. The relentless bombing campaign all but ceased for many years, allowing the city centre to come back to life. No longer subject to body searches, citizens were able to pour in and out of the security gates at will. Bright shops and boutiques blossomed, and flower tubs, thousands of trees, new paving and modern lamp standards adorned the main streets. Between 1982 and 1985 forty-one restaurants, thirty-eight cafés and fifty-five hot-food bars opened. Around £86 million was invested in commercial development in the inner city between 1983 and 1985 and it is estimated that in 1984 alone daytrippers from the Republic of Ireland spent £120 million in Northern Ireland, much of it in Belfast.

John DeLorean in the car that bore his name. As part of its drive to stimulate the failing local economy, the government invested £80 million in DeLorean's high-profile venture to set up a car factory in Dunmurry with the specific intention of making skilled jobs available to west Belfast. The venture failed, and after much controversy, the factory closed on 31 May 1982. The 1985 Robert Zemeckis film *Back to the Future* made the DeLorean sports car a cult object by converting it into a time machine, but it appeared on the screens three years too late.

BELFAST TELEGRAPH

Much of this regeneration was heavily subsidised by the government and before the end of the decade a succession of tall post-modernist commercial premises and office blocks began to dominate the skyline. Before the end of 1981 the government had agreed to make housing its first social priority; the decision was made to breach the Matthew Stop Line and build in the green belt, and two thousand new homes went up at Poleglass. Much of the city was transformed by the Northern Ireland Housing Executive's developments, imaginatively and harmoniously designed. 'An outsider who has not visited the city for two or three years would notice the difference right away,' Billy Simpson wrote in the *Belfast Telegraph* on 13 May 1985. 'A new buzz and bustle about a Belfast that suddenly looks better, smells better and smiles easier. A city on its way back.'

DeLorean sports cars in receivership in the premises of Harland and Wolff. David Beresford of the *Guardian* described the demise of the factory at Dunmurry: 'The funeral, such as it was, passed off uneventfully. The obsequies were performed by the 1,500 workers and the Department of Health and Social Security who kept open two social security offices on the Bank Holiday, so the workers could sign on the dole . . .'

NMGNI UFTM

LEFT:
Sister Genevieve, principal of St Louise's Comprehensive College in west Belfast. Under her remarkable direction a small local school went on to become the largest girls' school in Europe. It was the only truly comprehensive school in all of Northern Ireland, until Lagan College and other integrated schools were given government support. The result was that girls, many from some of the most deprived homes in the city, were able to progress upwards to choose from a wide selection of A level subjects without moving school.

BBC NI

BELOW:
Staff and pupils of Lagan College in the school's first academic year of 1981–2, Church Road, Castlereagh. Though Catholics did attend some of Belfast's more prestigious state grammar schools, in practice primary and secondary education was rigidly segregated. A group of determined parents, convinced that separate education perpetuated divisions and limited understanding, set up Lagan College which began in a scout hut near Shaw's Bridge with 28 pupils in two classrooms separated by a curtain, and art classes were conducted in a garage amongst canoes. They made their first move in January 1982. For almost a decade integrated education had to survive on charitable support until Brian Mawhinney, the education minister, gave his wholehearted backing. The new building at Lisnabreeny was officially opened on 25 October 1991.

LAGAN COLLEGE

Volunteers of the Provisional IRA fire shots over the coffin of Bobby Sands, 7 May 1981. Sands, the Provisional IRA prisoners' officer commanding in the Maze, began refusing food on 1 March 1981 to press forward the campaign for the restoration of political status that had started in 1976 with the 'blanket protest'. Other IRA prisoners joined the hunger strike and on 9 April Sands was elected MP in a Fermanagh–South Tyrone by-election. He died on 5 May, the sixty-sixth day of his hunger strike. On the day of his funeral at least 100,000 people – nearly one fifth of the entire Catholic population of Northern Ireland – crowded the route from St Luke's church in Twinbrook to Milltown cemetery. Journalists present found the silence, broken only by a lone piper, awesome in so vast a throng of mourners. Nine others were to die in the hunger strike before it ended five months later.

BELFAST TELEGRAPH

Gerry Adams acknowledges the applause of his supporters at the Sinn Féin offices on the Falls Road, after being elected MP for West Belfast in the general election of June 1983. The standing of the Provisional IRA and its political wing, Sinn Féin, had risen spectacularly in Catholic enclaves during the H-Block hunger strikes. In this election Adams, then vice-president of Sinn Féin, defeated Gerry Fitt, in a 73 per cent turnout; 13.4 per cent of the electorate voted for Sinn Féin candidates.

VICTOR PATTERSON

LEFT:
Poleglass, a major housing development south-west of Belfast. The planning of this estate was dogged by controversy: loyalist Lisburn clamoured against the southward advance of a Catholic tidal wave through Protestant farmland; environmentalists objected to the destruction of part of the green belt; and planners worried that the abandonment of the Matthew Stop Line would create an unwieldy urban sprawl linking Lisburn directly to Belfast. However, there was a severe housing shortage in north and west Belfast where Catholics were clustered in dilapidated nineteenth-century houses. In November 1980 the first thirty families moved into Poleglass. Lessons from the past had been learned: particular attention was paid to good planning and design in order to promote a sense of community; and careful steps were taken to prevent squatting.

NI HOUSING EXECUTIVE

The peaceline between Ardoyne and Alliance Road. The first peaceline was at Cupar Street, a grim barrier of concrete reminiscent of the Berlin Wall, marking the volatile divide between the Shankill and the Falls. Eventually there were thirteen peacelines separating 1.2 per cent of houses in the city. Wide strips of no-man's-land and planted parks were useless as alternatives since they provided battle ground and cover for paramilitaries and, for those reasons, peacelines proved popular with residents of interface areas.

IRISH NEWS

Selling apples at St George's Market, 1982. The market never ceased to flourish every Tuesday and Friday during the darkest days of the Troubles. It is the best fish market in Belfast, with the produce of the Irish Sea brought fresh from Ardglass and Portavogie and laid out on big white trays; meat, fruit and vegetables are piled high; seedlings and bedding plants are spread neatly across the concrete floor; second-hand clothes hang from rails; and many absorbing hours can be spent looking over bric-à-brac and collectibles. The camaraderie of the traders is obvious and much of the attraction of the market is the unceasing banter between them and their customers.

BILL KIRK

Joy Street, in the Markets area, rebuilt in the 1980s. Charles Brett, chairman of the Northern Ireland Housing Executive and later its historian, declared in October 1980: 'The figures for overcrowding are just double those in Manchester, one of the worst housed cities in England.' Chris Patten, the housing minister in the Northern Ireland Office, agreed to increase government funding to the extent that the Executive was able to spend around £100 million a year by the mid-1980s. Thanks largely to the personal interest taken by Brett, some of the nineteenth-century houses were restored and others were sensitively built to blend in, making the street one of the most attractive in the city. Joy Street was once known as the 'street of the three Ps'– that is pride, poverty and pianos – as each house had a piano in the parlour for music hall performers lodging there. In 1906 and 1907 Charlie Chaplin stayed at number 24. St Malachy's Church stands in the background.

NI HOUSING EXECUTIVE

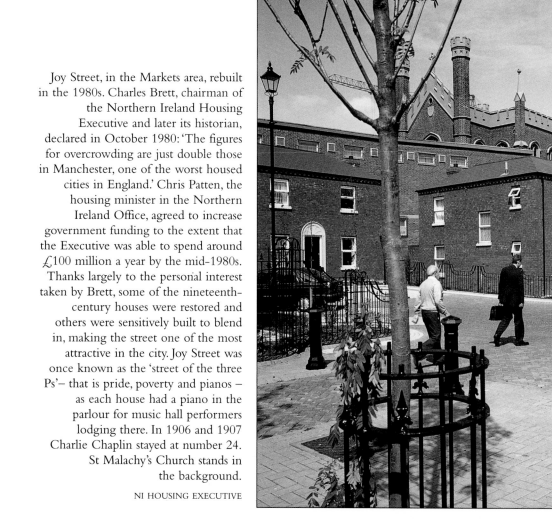

LEFT:

Punks in Cornmarket, 1983. By this time the city centre was coming back to life and, particularly on Saturday afternoons and at night, young people thronged the hot-food bars, fast-food restaurants and public houses in the main shopping area, Great Victoria Street, the Dublin Road and Shaftesbury Square.

BILL KIRK

BELOW:

Spectators await the passing of Orange bands on the Lisburn Road on 12 July 1983. From early morning every year bands collect from Protestant districts all over Belfast, together with visiting bands from Scotland and elsewhere, and converge on the city centre and march south to the 'Field', which on this occasion was at Finaghy. In a divided city there are divided opinions on this Twelfth march: for many Catholics it is triumphalist and threatening, but for most Protestants it is a day of festive celebration and historic pageantry. The Twelfth in Belfast is certainly one of the largest annual parades in Europe and it takes many hours for the fife and drum bands, kilted pipers, silver and brass bands, and accordion players, accompanied by bowler-hatted Orangemen wearing collarettes, painted banners, horse-drawn carriages and 'Billy' boys and girls cheering on their favourite lodges to pass down the Lisburn Road.

BILL KIRK

180

OPPOSITE TOP:
The hot summer of 1983 on Botanic Avenue. This street, from Shaftesbury Square, past Queen's University to the Botanic Gardens, witnessed a notable revival in this decade. Audiences returned to the Arts Theatre, delicatessens and other specialist shops opened, the street acquired a wide choice of good restaurants, a large new hotel was built on the corner of University Street, and a series of fashionable bars appealed mainly to the young and fancy free – the City Temple in this photograph changed its allegiance from God to Mammon and became the Empire Bar soon afterwards. A combination of the Troubles, a fall in church membership and the movement of people to live on the outskirts brought about the closure of several city centre churches.

BILL KIRK

A cross being carried into St Peter's Pro-Cathedral by members of Glenand Youth and Community Workshop, Easter 1988. Even after the completion of Divis Tower close by in 1972, the twin spires of St Peter's remain a distinctive landmark.

IRISH NEWS

The statue of St Patrick being removed from its pedestal at the front of St Patrick's Church in Donegall Street. St Patrick's was Belfast's second Catholic church and much of the cost of the original building was paid for by Protestant subscription. The original 1812 building was replaced by a Gothic Revival church in red sandstone in 1877. It is thought probable that this statue of the patron saint was sculpted by the English stonemason father of Patrick Pearse, the leader of the 1916 Easter rising in Dublin.

IRISH NEWS

ABOVE:

The massive unionist protest against the Anglo-Irish Agreement on the afternoon of Saturday 23 November 1985. Having failed to get a satisfactory replacement for the power-sharing executive of 1974, the British government came to an agreement with Dublin, which included an intergovernmental conference serviced by a permanent secretariat of northern and southern civil servants at Maryfield in Belfast. Ian Paisley's Democratic Unionist Party and the Ulster Unionists led by James Molyneaux joined together to pledge resistance to the 'diktat', the accord made without their involvement. Estimates of the numbers present that afternoon vary but they may have reached more than 200,000. The slogan of the unionist campaign was 'Ulster Says No', and Belfast City Council voted to raise a huge banner in front of the City Hall with the words, 'Belfast Says No'.

BELFAST TELEGRAPH

RIGHT:

Taking down the 'Belfast Says No' banner from the front of the City Hall in 1995.

IRISH NEWS

Lone loyalist Michael Stone firing at mourners in Milltown cemetery on 16 March 1988. Three members of the Provisional IRA had been shot dead in Gibraltar ten days earlier by the SAS. Stone infiltrated the crowds of sympathisers at the funerals; he threw three home-made hand grenades and fired shots, killing three people and injuring several others before being overpowered by the police. Three days later television cameras captured the full, chilling horror of what happened at the funeral of one of Stone's victims: a furious crowd closed in on the car of two corporals in civilian clothes who had strayed into the funeral cortège. The soldiers were dragged away and later stripped, beaten and shot dead beside Andersonstown Leisure Centre.

PACEMAKER

RIGHT:
The triumphant return on 10 June 1985 of Barry McGuigan, who had thrilled millions by defeating Eusebio Pedroza in a fifteen-round contest in London to become the new featherweight boxing champion of the world. 'Belfast, the divided city where Barry trained and filled boxing arenas with fight fans of every religious shade, showed how to lay on a real welcome,' the *Daily Mirror* observed. In Royal Avenue McGuigan mounted a float decked out like a boxing ring; he held his infant son Blaine aloft to deafening cheers and his wife Sandra waved and smiled. While his ebullient manager Barney Eastwood handed out bottles of champagne, Barry toasted his supporters with a glass of orange juice. At one point the lord mayor hoisted the boxer aloft and he in return lifted Alderman John Carson deftly into the air to rapturous applause.

BELFAST TELEGRAPH

BELOW:
On 18 April 1982 Bangor beat Carrick at Ravenhill to become winners of rugby's Ulster Senior Cup.

ESLER CRAWFORD

Camogie, 1984. Queen's University's Yvonne Redmond dashes in but Joan Gormley beats her to the ball to score for University College Dublin.

IRISH NEWS

Dog racing at Celtic Park in 1982. This track, the first in Ireland, opened on Easter Monday 1927 and later another track was set up at Dunmore. For many years this was an immensely popular sport: dozens of men could be seen walking greyhounds before breakfast in the Woodvale and Falls parks and on race days trams were lined up to take punters and other devotees to and from the meetings. This working-class pursuit cut across sectarian barriers ('there was never a word,' punters remember) and had its own special atmosphere and lore delightfully celebrated in Sam McAughtry's short stories. The outbreak of the Troubles dealt dog racing a mortal blow and, though it was revived for a time by Sean Graham and others, the tracks had closed by early 1997: the Park Centre was built on the Celtic Park site and Dunmore Park has yet to be put to an alternative use.

BILL KIRK

Liam Neeson in the Field Day production of Brian Friel's *Translations*, at the Grand Opera House, shortly after the newly restored theatre reopened in 1980. The Ballymena-born actor worked in the Lyric Theatre in Belfast and the Abbey in Dublin before moving into films, including *The Bounty, The Mission, Rob Roy, Michael Collins, Star Wars: Episode 1 The Phantom Menace,* and most memorably as Oskar Schindler in *Schindler's List* in 1993, for which he received an Academy Award nomination for best actor.

BELFAST TELEGRAPH

BELOW:
Kenneth Branagh and Brid Brennan being filmed for BBC Northern Ireland's *Too Late to Talk to Billy* by Graham Reid, shown as a *Play for Today* on network television in February 1982. Branagh was born in Belfast but moved to live in England at a young age. He retained an affection for his native city, returning to it many times to speak and perform. Graham Reid has a remarkably sharp ear for Belfast speech patterns and draws on memories of his 'Village' childhood and employment as a hospital worker.

BBC NI

LEFT:
A fiddle workshop with the doyen of traditional players, Sean Maguire, at St Paul's School on the Falls Road in 1983.

BILL KIRK

BELOW:
Van Morrison emerged in the 1960s as perhaps the finest white rhythm and blues singer and songwriter in the British Isles. His early years in Belfast remain a constant source of inspiration and were most completely celebrated in *Astral Weeks*, and throughout his career his work refers to specific locations such as Fitzroy Avenue, Sandy Row, Cyprus Avenue and other places in Belfast. His explorations included Irish traditional music and in 1988 he collaborated with The Chieftains in the highly successful *Irish Heartbeat*.

BBC NI

A view of the city looking down the River Lagan towards Belfast Lough in a north-easterly direction. It was along the estuary and in the docklands that the most striking alterations were made to the city in the last decade of the twentieth century. Right foreground, the Ozone sports complex in Ormeau Park; new apartment blocks across the road from the park on the right bank of the river; left foreground, the Gasworks site where the Halifax Group is to invest £45 million and create around 1,500 jobs to expand its remote distribution capabilities; centre, the Waterfront Hall, the Hilton Hotel and the British Telecom Riverside Tower; just downstream of the Waterfront Hall, the Lagan Weir and Lookout, and the Dargan M3 bridge opened in 1994; and towards the lough on the right, Harland and Wolff with its cranes Samson and Goliath .

ESLER CRAWFORD

1990s

T HE LOOK OF BELFAST HAD IMPROVED MARKEDLY by the start of the 1990s but plans to prepare the city for the new millennium were marred by violence and political uncertainty. Finding it more difficult to target members of the security forces, the IRA intensified its campaign of bombs and murders. Massive explosive devices made of artificial fertiliser and Semtex wreaked havoc in Bedford Street, Shaftesbury Square, Glengall Street and elsewhere. Loyalist paramilitaries stepped up their killing of known republicans and increased the assassination of Catholics at random. Republican murders became more overtly sectarian and as a terrifying cycle of tit-for-tat assassination developed, stark fear enveloped housing estates all over the city and its periphery. Taxi drivers – operating one of the most courteous and inexpensive services available in any western European city – were fatally vulnerable in this sectarian war. Then, following large public demonstrations organised by the trade unions and joint political initiatives by London and Dublin, the IRA ordered a cessation of violence at the end of August 1994 and the loyalist paramilitaries joined together to announce their own ceasefire in October.

Mutual distrust proved difficult to dislodge and progress towards new political arrangements seemed agonisingly slow. Nevertheless, as police officers cast aside their flak jackets and military patrols disappeared from the streets, there was a gradual recognition that a new era in the city's history was arriving and the visit of President Bill Clinton in November 1995 was the occasion of a universal celebration of that fact. The IRA ceasefire was broken for a time, and brutal paramilitary shootings and beatings continued, but neither the paramilitaries nor their political representatives could ignore the citizens' profound desire for peace. Seemingly interminable negotiations finally resulted in the Good Friday Agreement at Stormont in 1998, subsequently ratified decisively by referendum.

A distinct change in atmosphere could be found in Belfast City Council. Journalist David McKittrick had written his impression of debates there in 1988: 'The sides sit, implacable and

Irish president, Mary Robinson gets a hug from a resident of Short Strand during her visit to the city in September 1996. This was a less controversial visit than the one she made three years earlier, when loyalist protesters and unionists expressed their anger when she shook the hand of Sinn Féin president Gerry Adams. Her election as president of the Republic in 1990, and the subsequent growth of her popularity, demonstrated that a sea change was taking place in southern Irish society.

IRISH NEWS

irreconcilable, just feet away from each other, each regarding compromise as defeat. Together they make up a bitter frozen little tableau.' A decade later unionist and republican councillors in committee discussed practical day-to-day municipal issues without incessant jibes and raised voices. In 1999 Bob Stoker, the Ulster Unionist lord mayor, and Marie Moore, the Sinn Féin deputy lord mayor, attended functions together, even if they avoided sitting at the same table. Thoroughly cleaned of grime accumulated over nearly a century and surrounded with attractive new railings, the City Hall looked as fresh as it had been when it had first opened in 1906.

Nowhere was the transformation of Belfast more apparent than by the banks of the river. The Laganside Corporation was charged with the task of applying a combination of public money and private investment to regenerate the docklands. From Ormeau Bridge down to the sea, well-lit walkways were constructed; a project conceived in the 1970s was realised at last when on the site of the old cattle and fish markets the Waterfront Hall was built to give citizens a concert hall and conference centre without rival in Ireland; nearby the British Telecom Riverside Tower and a new Hilton Hotel demonstrated the confidence of investors from outside; a rapid rise in prices for new apartments by the river showed that the people had equal confidence in the future of their city; and the Dargan Bridge, opened in 1994, smoothed the flow of traffic, particularly from north to east. As the final weeks of the second millennium approached, the people of Belfast could see the £91 million Odyssey complex begin to take shape to provide a 10,000-seat arena, a science centre, an IMAX theatre and a pavilion on a 23-acre site. At the same time plans to develop Titanic Park, on sixty acres next to Odyssey, as an information technology centre were well advanced, and news came through that the Halifax would create a call centre providing around 1,500 jobs at Cromac Wood in the regenerated Gasworks site. All this seemed to underscore the prediction that the return of peace would inaugurate a new period of recovery, prosperity and hope for the people of Belfast.

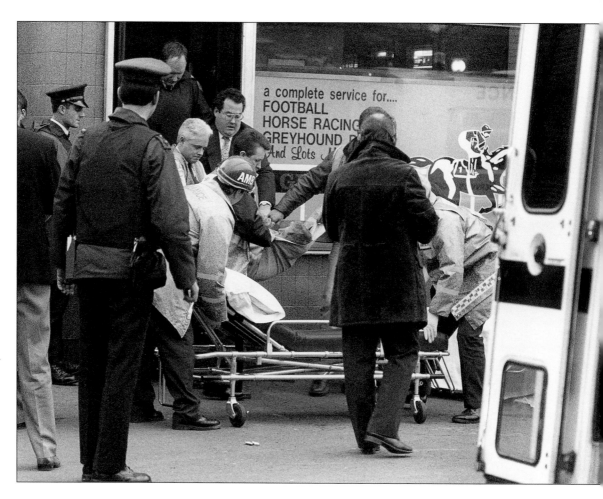

Sean Graham's betting shop on the lower Ormeau Road after a loyalist assassination attack on 5 February 1992. Just after 2 p.m. two men burst through the door with an automatic rifle and a pistol and fired indiscriminately at close range. Five Catholics were killed and seven more were wounded. The Ulster Freedom Fighters claimed responsibility and stated that the atrocity had been carried out in retaliation for the murder of eight Protestants at Teebane in County Tyrone on 17 January. More civilians had died in 1991 than in any year since 1976, and the toll for 1992 reached thirty-one by the end of February.

PACEMAKER

Frizzell's fish shop on the Shankill Road after two Provisionals had planted a bomb there at lunchtime on Saturday 23 October 1993. Altogether nine innocent civilians were killed along with Thomas Begley, one of the bombers. The IRA believed that the upstairs room was the west Belfast Ulster Defence Association headquarters. The bomb had exploded prematurely but it was revealed subsequently that casualties were unavoidable as the timing device could be set only for a maximum of eleven seconds.

PACEMAKER

LEFT:
In the spring of 1993 journalists revealed that John Hume, leader of the SDLP, had been having regular discussions with Gerry Adams, the president of Sinn Féin who had lost his West Belfast seat in 1992. The two men issued a joint statement on 24 April signalling that they were not prepared to go back to past political structures at Stormont. Hume was vilified by unionists but was convinced this way of searching for peace was the right one.

PACEMAKER

BELOW:
Ballynafeigh Orangemen hold a religious service on Ormeau Bridge on 28 April 1996, during one of several stand-offs when they had been refused permission to march over the bridge to the city centre. The lower Ormeau had become a Catholic enclave and protests from residents persuaded the authorities to stop parades going through the district. In the second half of the nineties the conflict increasingly was expressed in disputes over parade routes.

PACEMAKER

RIGHT:
Gusty Spence (foreground) who had been
jailed on a murder charge in the 1960s,
speaking during the announcement of the
Combined Loyalist Military Command's
ceasefire on 13 October 1994. During the
press conference in north Belfast Spence
read out a long ceasefire statement which
included an expression of remorse for the
killing of innocent victims

PACEMAKER

BELOW:
People in Andersonstown celebrate the
announcement of the IRA ceasefire. A succession of
murders and Sinn Féin's negative response to the
British government's 'clarification' of the December
1993 Downing Street Declaration had helped to
maintain an air of gloom over the summer of 1994,
which marked the twenty-fifth anniversary of troops
being put on active service in Northern Ireland. For
most citizens, therefore, the ceasefire announcement
was a bolt from the blue. At 11 a.m. on 31 August
1994 the media received this statement: 'The IRA
have decided that as of midnight, 31 August, there
will be a complete cessation of military operations.
All our units have been instructed accordingly.'

IRISH NEWS

LEFT:
US president Bill Clinton acknowledges a rapturous reception at the City Hall on the night of 30 November 1995. The city was at peace and the easing of tension since the autumn of 1994 had been palpable. However, in the search for new political arrangements a protracted stalemate had followed and Clinton was eager to do all he could to move the peace process on. In the bitter cold, tens of thousands packed Donegall Square, Donegall Place, and the streets stretching away from them, to give the Clintons a welcome they would never forget.

PACEMAKER

ABOVE:
Sinn Féin activists protest in front of Stormont at the exclusion of their party from talks in 1996.

IRISH NEWS

LEFT:
David Trimble was elected leader of the Ulster Unionist Party in September 1995. At the time he appeared more hard-line than his predecessor, James Molyneaux: he had been a Convention member for South Belfast for the Vanguard Unionist Progressive Party between 1975 and 1976; he had been associated for a time with the Ulster Clubs movement; after joining the Unionist Party in 1978, he had been elected for Upper Bann in 1990 and his triumphalism after the Drumcree march of July 1995 delighted loyalists. Thereafter, however, he was to show a willingness to consider all options which led him to play a key role in bringing about the Good Friday Agreement of 1998.

PACEMAKER

The Very Reverend Jack Shearer, the Church of Ireland dean of Belfast, on his annual sitout in 1998, the thirteenth successive year in which he had remained outside St Anne's Cathedral for seven days and nights to collect money for charity. A great many parents have brought their children to see the 'Black Santa' during Christmas shopping expeditions. In 1998 he raised more than £210,000 during the week, £55,000 coming in on 23 and 24 December for Christian Aid. The dean said that a 'lovely aspect of the sitout is the way in which it receives support from every section of the community. During the week contributions came from right across the board, including not only Protestants and Roman Catholics but also a number from non-Christian faiths.'

THE DEAN OF BELFAST

Father Peter McCann and solicitor Denis Moloney at the official opening of St Anne's Square opposite St Anne's Cathedral in Donegall Street in 1992. This square, which cost £1.7 million, proved an attractive upgrading to a previously derelict area in the heart of the city. Earlier in the year the priest and the lawyer lost a court battle to prevent a multi-storey Department of the Environment complex from being built in front of St Malachy's Church on Alfred Street.

IRISH NEWS

Sister Mary Olive, with her cat Whiskers, and Sister Mary Antoinette, at the blessing of the animals at St Joseph's in Pilot Street in May 1990.

IRISH NEWS

A diminutive patron saint during a St Patrick's Day parade on the Falls Road. At the beginning of the century the great majority of Protestants, including their elected representatives, unhesitatingly regarded themselves as being Irish, and members of the Church of Ireland, in particular, keenly celebrated the patron saint and identified with the precepts of the early Celtic Church – they dedicated their church on the lower Newtownards Road, with the largest congregation in Ireland, to St Patrick. As the century progressed, however, most Protestants felt themselves to be British and the marking of St Patrick's Day on 17 March was largely left to Catholics. Recent attempts to augment the festivities on St Patrick's Day, held in the city centre and with pageantry to attract both sides of the community, have met with only limited success.

IRISH NEWS

RIGHT:
'Uncle Kwong' of the Sun Kee Chinese restaurant in Donegall Pass. The Chinese form the largest ethnic minority group in Northern Ireland and number around 7,000. The great majority came from the New Territories, Hong Kong's rural area. Most live in Belfast and work in the catering business – the first Chinese restaurant in Belfast was set up in 1962. Many went to England, Scotland and the Irish Republic when the Troubles began but after the worst years had passed, their numbers began to rise again. Cantonese is the main language spoken.

NICEM/DEREK SPEIRS/REPORT

BELOW:
Friday prayer at the Belfast Islamic Centre, Wellington Park. Muslim children are encouraged to pray from the age of eight and prayer is obligatory from the age of twelve. 'People look at minorities as immigrants, that they are just here temporarily,' Dr Mamoun Mobayed of the centre has observed. 'They do not appreciate that people were born here, they live here and will die here. This is their home.' Apart from English, the most common languages amongst Muslims in the city are Malay, Arabic and Urdu.

NICEM/DEREK SPEIRS/REPORT

The Indian Community Centre in Clifton Street in 1993. A few Indians came to Belfast in the 1930s but it was not until the 1950s that larger numbers arrived. The first to come were men who sold clothes door-to-door, or took up a trade or set themselves up in business, and then returned to India to bring back their wives and families. By the 1990s most families in the city are second or third generation and they make a notable contribution to the urban economy as owners of factories, restaurants and other businesses, and as medical practitioners, broadcasters and other professionals. The centre was set up in 1981 and aims to maintain the culture and traditions of India, to provide social contact between members of the community, to provide opportunities for cultural and religious activities, to foster a women's group and to run classes in mother tongue languages, Hindi and Punjabi in particular.

BILL KIRK

Glen Road, west Belfast: as in the rest of Ireland, Travellers in Belfast have encountered hostility from settled citizens and have suffered from a host of ill-formed opinions. They form a distinct and separate group with a history going back for centuries. From the 1950s many of their sources of income disappeared, including tin-smithing, chimney cleaning, horse-dealing and selling domestic wares. Today they deal in scrap, bric-à-brac, antiques and caravans, and are engaged in tarmacking and carpentry.

NICEM/DEREK SPEIRS/REPORT

Stephen Rea, one of Belfast's most distinguished actors. Born Graham Rea in 1946, he began his acting career with Dramsoc at Queen's University. He had many stage and television parts before his film début in Neil Jordan's *Angel*, and in 1992 he played a tortured republican in Jordan's *The Crying Game*, for which he received an Academy Award nomination as best actor. He was a founder-member of the Field Day Theatre Company.

BELFAST TELEGRAPH

Sam McAughtry (left) and Paddy Devlin in the Kitchen Bar, 1994. McAughtry established himself as a writer of distinction with *The Sinking of the Kenbane Head*, an account of his upbringing in Tiger's Bay and of the death of his brother in a vessel sunk in the North Atlantic convoys. Possessing an unerring ear for Belfast speech, he has written numerous short stories and a novel. Paddy Devlin, interned between 1942 and 1945 for IRA membership, turned his back on militant republicanism to become active in the labour and trade union movement. He was chairman of the Northern Ireland Labour Party (1967–8), and in 1970 he was a founder-member of the SDLP, but was later expelled for his socialist views. He died in August 1999.

BBC NI

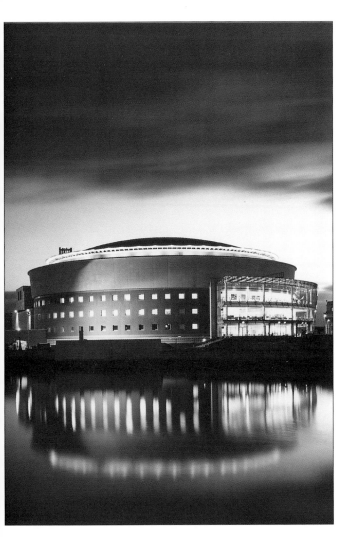

LEFT:

Designed by Victor Robinson, the Waterfront Hall opened its doors in 1997. The main auditorium – the largest of its kind in Ireland – accommodates 2,235 in tiered seating offering unrestricted views of the stage, with sound, lighting and suspension systems as comprehensive and sophisticated as any in the country. Patrons get splendid views of the river and the city from the upstairs cafés, bars and balconies. In addition, there are exhibition areas, the BT Studio, with seating for 450, and 17 smaller rooms.

BELFAST CITY COUNCIL

BELOW:

The Hole in the Wall Gang was created by three Belfast lawyers who became writer–performers, Damon Quinn, Tim McGarry and Michael McDowell. Their live performances in the Empire were hugely successful and in 1990 they won a wider audience with their award-winning six-week show *Perforated Ulster*, broadcast on BBC Radio Ulster. The following year their hard-hitting satire *Two Ceasefires and a Wedding* won the Royal Television Society Award for best regional programme. *Give My Head Peace*, their surreal comedy series which also confronts sectarianism and violence, has won a loyal and delighted audience.

BBC NI

Left to right: Taoiseach Bertie Ahern, former US senator George Mitchell and Prime Minister Tony Blair at Stormont after the signing of the Good Friday Agreement in April 1998. Mitchell won admiration from all sides for his patience, charm and diplomatic skills: he had chaired an international body on paramilitary arms decommissioning which reported in January 1996 and he was called back repeatedly to restart talks when they had stalled. Blair had come to Belfast only two weeks after his election victory – his first visit outside London. No British prime minister had ever devoted so much time and concentrated energy to seeking a solution for Northern Ireland. Ahern displayed similar commitment, breaking off his involvement only to attend his mother's funeral in Dublin.

IRISH NEWS

David Trimble (left), Bono and John Hume acknowledging tumultuous applause from a young audience at the Waterfront Hall in May 1998. The Yes campaign for the Good Friday Agreement appeared to be faltering coming up to the referendum on the deal on 22 May. The concert was the outcome of a telephone call to Tim Attwood of the SDLP from Paul Hewson – better known as Bono of U2 – asking whether he could help. Attwood got promoter Eamonn McCann to arrange the concert featuring U2 and Ash, a young group from Downpatrick. More than 71 per cent of the Northern Ireland electorate ratified the agreement and the *Belfast Telegraph*, in its special late poll edition on 23 May, ran a headline: 'U2 concert derailed No camp's train'.

IRISH NEWS

ABOVE:
Luciano Pavarotti performs at Stormont in September 1999 with the Ulster Orchestra. The great tenor made his début in the United Kingdom as Lieutenant Pinkerton in *Madam Butterfly* at Belfast's Grand Opera House in 1963. Secretary of State Mo Mowlam instigated the use of the grounds at Stormont as a concert venue with a performance by Elton John on 27 May 1998, just days after the Good Friday Agreement had been endorsed by referendums north and south.

IRISH NEWS

Mo Mowlam meets the media. As Northern Ireland secretary of state, her unflagging determination to encourage politicians to reach agreement, her willingness to engage in discussion with everyone, her courage in meeting prisoners in the Maze in the face of intense criticism, her evident warmth and her informal style with journalists won her admiration from a very wide range of people. Unionists, however, became increasingly suspicious of her intentions and called for her replacement. In a cabinet reshuffle in October 1999 she was replaced by Peter Mandelson.

PACEMAKER

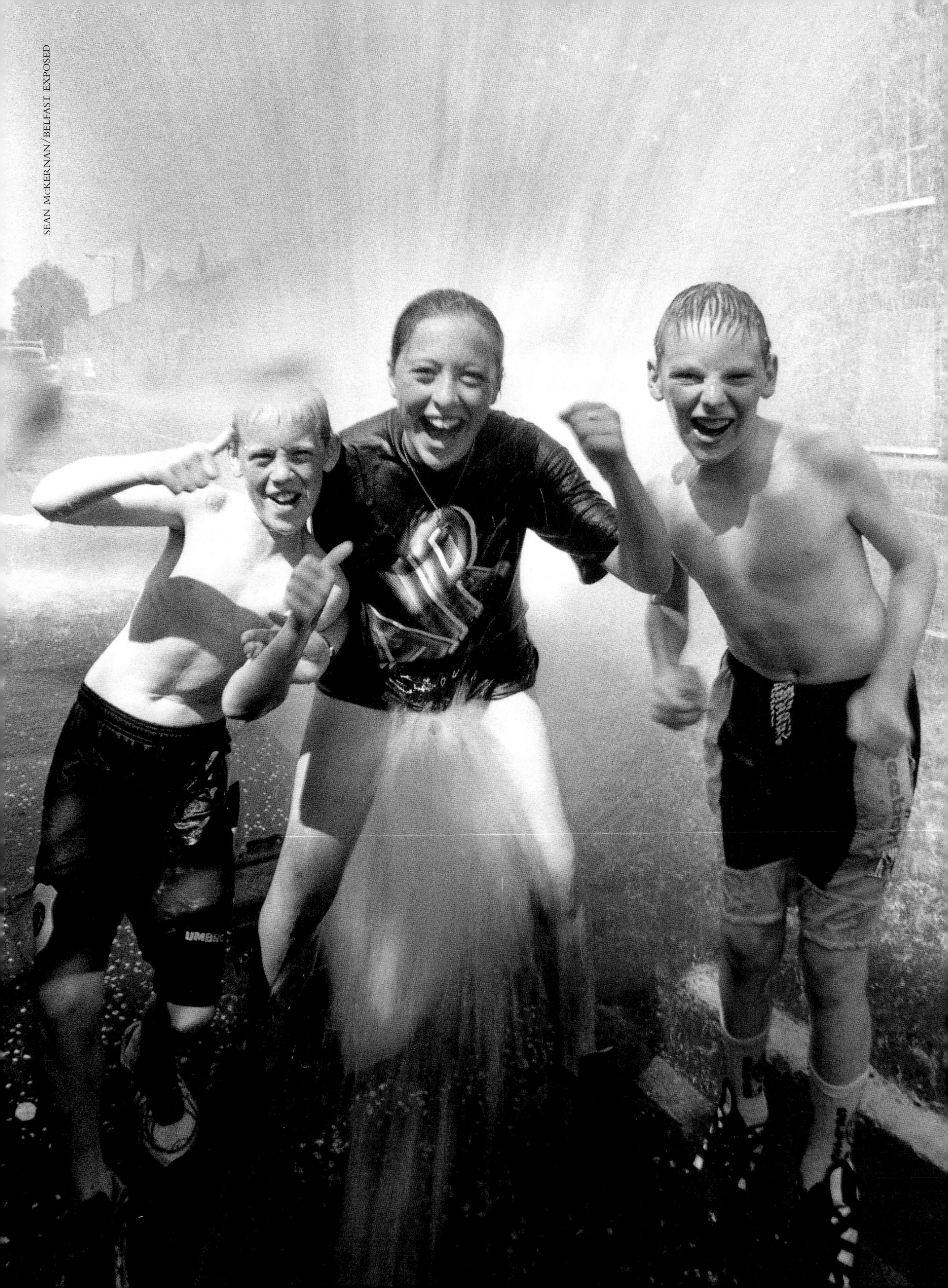

SEAN McKERNAN/BELFAST EXPOSED